Twenty-First Century Corporate Reporting

Twenty-First Century Corporate Reporting

Effective Use of Technology and the Internet

Gerald Trites

BEP

BUSINESS EXPERT PRESS

Leader in applied, concise business books

Twenty-First Century Corporate Reporting:
Effective Use of Technology and the Internet

Copyright © Business Expert Press, LLC, 2021.

Cover design by Charlene Kronstedt

Interior design by Exeter Premedia Services Private Ltd., Chennai, India

First published in 2021 by
Business Expert Press, LLC
222 East 46th Street, New York, NY 10017
www.businessexpertpress.com

ISBN-13: 978-1-63742-068-3 (paperback)
ISBN-13: 978-1-63742-069-0 (e-book)

Business Expert Press Financial Accounting, Auditing, and Taxation Collection

Collection ISSN: 2151-2795 (print)
Collection ISSN: 2151-2817 (electronic)

First edition: 2021

10 9 8 7 6 5 4 3 2 1

Description

How and why do corporations use the internet for reporting to their stakeholders? How and why has corporate reporting extended beyond financial reporting to include environmental, social, and governance (ESG) reporting and even integrated reporting. The major drivers of modern reporting have changed, to include data driven decision making, big data, and advanced analytics, as well as the use of electronic representations of data with tools such as XBRL.

Here we explore the various vehicles for using the internet, including social media and blogs as well as corporate websites and the websites of regulators. And we delve into the impact of portable devices, like smartphones and tablets.

Corporate reporting on the internet is changing fast because of changes in technology and stakeholder expectations. Companies are having a hard time keeping up. This book offers a roadmap to follow—a roadmap to start on now. Most importantly, the book lays out a strong case for integrated reporting and shows how reporting on the internet is ideally suited to the creation of integrated reports.

This book is of interest to executives in charge of the reporting function for their companies, students of accounting and management, and to serious investors and others with a strong interest in corporate reporting and the direction in which it is headed.

Keywords

business reporting; financial reporting; financial reports; XBRL; iXBRL; big data; governance reporting; environmental reporting; ESG reporting; Internet use; social media; reporting on the Internet; big data; graphics; integrated reporting

Contents

Preface

The purpose of this book is to provide a comprehensive overview of corporate reporting on the Internet, including the websites of the reporting companies, regulators, intermediaries, and social media. It should be of particular interest to advanced students of accounting, finance, and corporate administration. In addition, the book will be of interest to people responsible for some or all of the corporate reporting function who work in public companies and any others interested in how and why companies use the Internet to report their affairs, and indeed their impact on society, to the public. It is not restricted to purely financial matters. For example, there is a strong emphasis on how companies report on their impact on the environment, society, and governance and the concluding chapters offer some clear ideas as to the direction companies should take in their reporting function.

This publication was prepared with the help of several talented people who agreed to review the material at different stages of its development. My profound thanks go to Roger Debreceny PhD, Eric Cohen CPA, Don Sheehy CPA, Alan Willis FCPA, and Alex Young CPA. I also offer my gratitude to Gundi Jeffrey and Margaret MacDonald Trites for their excellent editing and proofreading services. Any remaining errors or shortcomings are entirely my responsibility.

G Trites

Introduction

At present, most public companies use the Internet as a prime vehicle for corporate reporting. Most of them still provide paper reports and in some jurisdictions, they are required to do so, but the main vehicle of reporting has shifted to the Internet. Most of the companies have Investor Relations (IR) sections of their websites designated to provide financial and business reports.

History of Reporting on the Internet

Financial reporting by companies and other organizations has historically been carried out by means of paper reports, but in and around the year 2000, this began to change. At that time, the Internet was in its infancy, and the World Wide Web even more so, having just been invented by Sir Timothy Berners-Lee in 1989. Although many people could see a lot of potential in the Web, they were just beginning to explore its uses.

Several studies of corporate websites were done at that time, notably through the Canadian Institute of Chartered Accountants (CICA, now CPA Canada), the International Accounting Standards Board (IASB), and the American Institute of Certified Public Accountants (AICPA). The studies looked into the question of what use companies were making of the Internet for financial reporting purposes. The studies all revealed that although some companies had posted part or all of their latest financial statements on the Web, many had not. In addition, numerous public companies were found to not even have a website.

The CICA's report, titled "The Impact of Technology on Financial Reporting," released in 1999, was the most comprehensive, being based on a random sample of 370 public companies drawn from the companies listed on the New York Stock Exchange, NASDAQ, and the Toronto Stock Exchange. A significant finding of the study was that only 255 of the 370 companies had websites at the end of 1998. Of these, only 129 disclosed some financial information on their sites and only

95 companies included a full set of financial statements, including a Balance Sheet, Statement of Income, Statement of Changes in Financial Position (or equivalent), and Notes to the Financial Statements.

Most of those who had posted their financial statements did little else in terms of financial reporting on the Web, so financial reporting on the Web at that time was considered something very much optional, something additional to the "real" reporting activity, which was carried out through paper means. Financial statements at that time, as at present, were usually included in the Annual Report of the company.

Since the turn of the century, additional studies have been carried out; for example, a 2010 study in Management Accounting Quarterly stated: "Our study discovered all Fortune 100 companies had websites."[1] (No surprise there.) It is noteworthy that this study used as its sample all Fortune 100 companies whereas the CICA study used a random sample of public companies. Therefore, the results are not entirely comparable. But they do provide an overview of the general trends taking place. The study went on to state that "The Fortune 100 websites have emphasized the link to investor relations/financial information pages over the years, increasing the percentage of websites with such links from 75% in 2003 to 80% in 2006 and 97% in 2009."[2] Most Investor Relations sections of corporate websites now contain complete financial statements, and indeed in most cases, the complete Annual Report.

Finally, there has been much research exploring the apparent deteriorating usefulness of financial reporting. These studies have ranged from work on the relationship between financial reporting and stock market prices to the emerging variations in reporting of results of operations—variations from traditional net income measures to numerous non-GAAP measures that often reduce comparability and detract from the traditional measures. A major issue is whether reporting on the Internet has any effect on the usefulness of financial reporting.

Regulatory Requirements

Initially, regulators and standards-setting organizations were reluctant to recognize web-based financial reporting. This soon changed, however, and several of them released statements on the subject. One of the first was the U.S. Securities and Exchange Commission (SEC) which, on July 7, 2006, issued a release to say

> In recognition of the central role of the Internet in today's global economy, many companies rely on their corporate websites as basic information sources and marketing tools for business partners, customers and the general public. In light of increased attention to corporate governance matters and recent SEC and stock exchange corporate governance requirements, public companies typically create within their corporate websites a separate page devoted to investor relations, and many companies also create separate pages devoted exclusively to corporate governance matters, such as information about the board of directors and committees.[3]

The release summarized SEC, New York Stock Exchange (NYSE), and Nasdaq rules relating to website posting of SEC filings, corporate governance materials, and other items, and provided practical advice.

Currently, all public companies in the United States must file regular financial reports with the SEC. These reports include the annual report (i.e. the 10-K), quarterly reports (10-Q), and numerous other reports. The reports are filed through the SEC's Electronic Data Gathering, Analysis, and Retrieval system (EDGAR), which was phased in over a period from 1984 until 1996. All of the reports filed with the SEC can be found on the EDGAR website. Some companies have adopted the practice of using the 10-K required for filing with the SEC as their annual report. They wish to avoid the cost of preparing, printing, and distributing large annual reports, partially because most of the information that would be in a traditional annual report is already disclosed on the website.

In Canada, all publicly listed companies must file similar information with the Canadian Securities Administrators, using a tool somewhat similar to EDGAR, called SEDAR (System for Electronic Document Analysis and Retrieval), and the reports can be found on the SEDAR website at www.sedar.com.

In Britain, companies file their reports with Companies House, and in several other countries there are similar facilities. The European

Securities and Marketing Agency (ESMA) requires that companies listed on European exchanges must file their reports using a recently initiated standard referred to as "The European Single Electronic Format" (ESEF). This is the format in which issuers on European Union-regulated markets were required to prepare their annual financial reports for fiscal periods beginning on or after January 1, 2020, but this requirement was later optionally deferred for one year because of the pandemic. These filings occur at a national level, with public companies obliged to make their disclosures to OAMs ("Officially Appointed Mechanisms"). These are often national stock exchanges, frequently the securities regulator itself, and in some cases a trusted third party.

The IR Sections on websites contain more than financial information. The annual report of the company is only one component of contemporary reporting. There has been a growing recognition that traditional financial reports do not provide enough information for stakeholders to make many of the decisions they need to make. Investors and others realized that more information was required on the governance structure of the company as well as its social and environmental policies. So, companies began providing environmental, social, and governance (ESG) reports in addition to their Annual Report.

While the Annual Report is always included in the IR Section of the corporate websites, the ESG reports are sometimes excluded from the IR Section and placed in separate sections of the website either together or separately. This may change, however, because in 2020 the IFRS Foundation issued a consultation on establishing a sustainability standards board, which might change the predilection of separating financial from sustainability reporting; that is, toward integrated reporting.[4]

There has been a movement toward integrated reporting in recent years, which integrates the financial, social, governance, and environmental reporting into one single report. Some companies, such as Shell and Mitsubishi Corporation, have initiated this approach. While the concept of integrated reporting is simple, the execution of the concept has been found to be somewhat difficult for companies to implement. The problem lies in the difference between integrating and combining. True integration involves working through the reports line by line and integrating the various elements of reporting (Financial and ESG) into presentations that take all such viewpoints into account. Most so-called integrated reports issued to date simply combine the elements but do not integrate them. Reporting on the Internet, however, is ideally suited to integrating material through the use of weblinks. Chapters 9 and 10 explore this idea.

Corporate reporting, including financial and other business disclosure, is essentially a process of communication between the company and its stakeholders. As such, the company must assess the needs of the stakeholders and determine the best means of effectively conveying the information they need.

The needs of the stakeholders vary greatly. Investors need information to help them make decisions as to whether to buy, hold, or sell. Creditors need to evaluate the ability of the company to repay their loans and take on new debts. Regulators need to ensure compliance with the relevant rules and legislation. Governments need to monitor compliance with governing legislation and evaluate the impact of the company on the areas under their jurisdiction for policy purposes. Customers and suppliers need to consider the stability of the company as a trading partner. And the public in general needs to evaluate the impact of the company on the economy and the environment.

The needs are broad and demanding. This book explains how the Internet can be used to meet these needs much more effectively.

CHAPTER 1

The Components of Corporate Reporting

Originally, corporate reporting was comprised of financial reporting, which in turn consisted of financial statements, but over the years, it has extended considerably beyond the financial statements and even beyond the annual report to include a variety of interim reports, regulatory reports, and statutory reports. Also, there is reporting in news and other releases that provides information on important events affecting the company, such as strikes, information system intrusions, fires, and earthquakes. Closely related is reporting on corporate actions, such as dividend announcements, earnings announcements, and capital restructuring such as stock splits and stock dividends. And more recently, corporate reporting has extended beyond financial reporting to include reporting on environmental, social, and governance (ESG) matters (Figure 1.1).

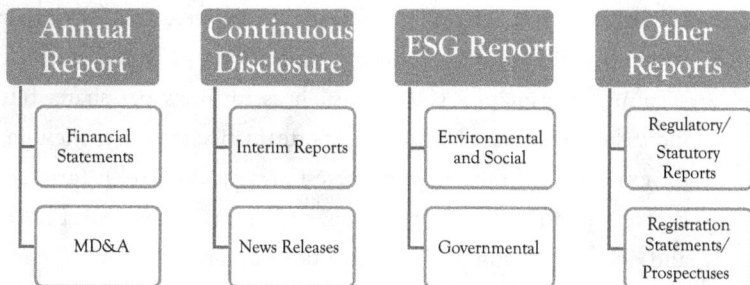

Figure 1.1 Components of corporate reporting

Annual Reports

A look at current annual reports reveals a number of additional items of information beyond the financial statements. Some of the more significant items are:

a. *The report/letter of the President or chief executive officer (CEO).* Although this is seldom a lengthy document, the CEO's report is often viewed as important for gaining an insight into the thinking of upper management and the CEO on major issues and the direction of the company.

b. *Forward-looking information.* While forward-looking information is included in several parts of the Investor Relations Section, there is often a section that draws it together and provides thoughts, estimates, forecasts, and prognostications on the future. Any predictions are usually provided with great care.

c. *Interim financial information.* Public companies are required by the regulators to file and provide to their shareholders interim financial reports, usually quarterly. Basic interim financial information is usually included in the annual report as well.

d. *Performance measures.* A growing aspect of corporate reporting has been the use of performance measures to provide useful metrics about the operations of the company. These appear in the annual report and also on the main page (quite often) of the IR Section of the website. These measures were usually drawn from information prepared in accordance with generally accepted accounting principles (GAAP), such as earnings per share, but increasingly are not. Non-GAAP performance measures include, for example, earnings before interest and taxes (EBIT); earnings before interest, taxes, depreciation, and amortization (EBITDA); and adjusted earnings. They have been an area of growing concern with standards setters and regulators because of their popularity and the lack of consistency of how non-GAAP measures are defined in filings and the possibility that investors might be misled.

Management Discussion and Analysis Reports

Some years ago, with the increased complexity of modern companies, investors realized that they needed more information from management to explain the financial statements.

As a result, the major regulators developed requirements for companies to prepare Management Discussion and Analysis (MD&A) reports, which include extensive narratives on management's analysis of the company's performance. The Securities and Exchange Commission (SEC) issued their initial guidance in 1987 and 1989. An MD&A report is usually included within a company's annual report. The MD&A can also include a discussion of compliance, risks, and plans. The MD&A section represents the thoughts and opinions of management and is not audited, but the major standard-setting bodies, such as the Financial Accounting Standards Board (FASB), have issued standards to be met.

MD&A Reports contain the following classes of information:

1. *Core Businesses*—including the company's business model, what the company does, the markets in which it operates, how it generates revenue and creates value.
2. *Objectives and Strategy*—including the major internal and external factors, opportunities, and risks considered by management in developing their strategy.
3. *Capability: Resources and Relationships*—including the capability of the company and each core business to execute strategy, manage activities, and achieve objectives. Also included are the nature and extent of relationships with other parties important to the company. This would include the entity's dependence on the parties, any management or board involvement with them, their financial implications, and any exposure to increased risk.
4. *Risks*—material risks to the company and their potential impact, including the company's strategy for managing those risks.
5. *Performance*—a discussion of the factors that affected past financial and operating performance and their relevance to future prospects. This includes an identification of the key performance

indicators used by management and their relevance to the company's goals.

6. *Outlook*—for the company as a whole and for each core business.

MD&As tend to explain these matters and others in considerable detail; indeed, investors and regulators have come to expect comprehensive discussions and detail in them.

Environmental, Social, and Governance Reports

Environmental, Social, and Governance (ESG) Reporting has become a very important part of corporate reporting in recent years, as the interests of stakeholders have broadened beyond purely financial interests. This broadening has been enhanced recently by financial considerations, since it has become clear that the environment poses serious financial risks emanating from such events as floods, fires, tidal waves, and extreme storms. As well, the environmental footprint of a company can have financial repercussions, such as fines, penalties, lawsuits, and costs incurred to upgrade or improve facilities to lessen that footprint. With these concerns, many stakeholders are demanding to know more about the environmental footprint of the company and its actions to prevent, or at least to minimize, any adverse effects the company might have on the environment as well as the adverse effects the environment might have on the company.

ESG reporting is largely about risk. In addition to environmental considerations, "it covers social issues like a company's labour practices, talent management, product safety and data security. It covers governance matters like board diversity, executive pay and business ethics."[1]

The governance report is usually quite extensive and outlines the structure and policies of the company pertaining to its governance. More specifically, it provides information on the composition of the Board of Directors and Board Committees and other committees, as well as their terms of reference and operating policies. The report provides the role and policies regarding the Annual Meeting and the Auditors. In many cases, information will be provided about the corporate whistleblower policies. While some companies provide what they call an ESG Report, most provide Environmental, Social, and Governance reports separately or as part of the annual report. Sometimes these reports are included as part of the Investor Relations section and in other cases are outside of it.

Interim Reports

Corporate reporting has traditionally been carried out on a periodic basis, primarily in the form of annual financial statements and annual reports. Accordingly, there arose a need for companies to issue interim reports to provide stakeholders with more current information about the financial results since the last annual report. Usually this has been done on a quarterly basis, and quarterly reports have been mandated by regulators such as the SEC and Ontario Securities Commission (OSC) for many years.

Some feel that the concept of interim reports is rapidly going out of date with the advent of the Web and other means of electronic reporting since stakeholders no longer need to wait for information until the end of the next quarter. For example, companies regularly put current information, such as news releases and announcements on their websites, and on Twitter and other social media. However, interim reports do have to follow established standards and formats and do provide useful information, particularly about earnings, so they remain an important component of financial reporting.

Interim financial reports started out as brief summaries of operations, consisting of a condensed income statement for the quarter and year to date presented in comparative form. Quarterly reports have grown since then and are now presented in the investor relations section of the website. For example, the quarterly report of the Bank of Montreal for the second quarter of 2020 extends to 90 pages and includes comprehensive notes and commentary on the results of operations during the quarter and year to date. The second quarterly report of 2020 for the Kraft Heinz Company extends to 191 pages and is a very comprehensive report to shareholders. In fact, the report is the 10-Q form that needs to be filed by public companies listed in the United States with the SEC.

Many U.S. listed companies have adopted the practice of using the SEC forms for their shareholder reports—the 10-Q for the quarterly reports and the 10-K for their annual reports. This is an unfortunate practice since the regulatory forms are not geared to be user-friendly. Therefore, the companies that follow this practice lose an opportunity to communicate effectively with their stakeholders. It would be much more effective for them to design and write a report with graphics and pictures that would attract interest and encourage reading and generally tell a more interesting story for their stakeholders.

Prospectuses

A major and complex form of corporate reporting is found in prospectuses. These are large reports required by securities commissions to be provided when a company goes public through an initial public offering (IPO) and when a company is already public and wishes to issue shares or other instruments to the public.

A prospectus includes a complete copy of the latest audited financial statements along with disclosures about the details and purpose of the particular offering, projections about financial results and details about the company, its management and organization. They are usually massive documents and are designed to provide in one place all the information that a potential investor would need to make an informed decision about investing.

Prospectuses are normally issued by a company in conjunction with a lawyer, the company's auditors, and an underwriter. All have distinct responsibilities and must sign letters of comfort, which offer some assurance to the users of their services that the signers have followed due process in discharging their duties.

In the United States, prospectuses must be filed with the SEC and are then included on Electronic Data Gathering, Analysis, and Research (EDGAR). In Canada, they are filed with the Securities Commissions of Canada and reported on System for Electronic Analysis and Retrieval (SEDAR). In this way, prospectuses become an important part of a company's corporate reporting on the Internet.

Continuous Disclosure and Reporting

Continuous Disclosure Requirements

Securities legislation sets out numerous requirements for continuous disclosure, the main elements of which include:

- Companies are required to file annual and interim financial statements which must be accompanied by the MD&A.
- Companies are encouraged to provide forward-looking information in the disclosures they provide to the public if they have a reasonable basis for doing so. The MD&A would almost automatically involve some of this, since the preparation of an MD&A necessarily involves some degree of prediction or projection. All forward-looking information must contain a statement that the information is forward-looking; a description of the factors that may cause actual results to differ materially from the forward-looking information; material assumptions; and appropriate risk disclosure and cautionary language.
- Some companies must file a government developed information form every year, usually some period after the end of the company's most recent financial year. It would provide material information about a company and its business in the context of its historical and possible future development.
- Any material changes to the company's affairs are required under securities legislation to be publicly disclosed through a filing and through press releases, including:
  - a change in the business, operations, or capital of a company that would reasonably be expected to have a significant effect on the market price or value of any of its securities;
  - a decision to implement such a change made by the board of directors or other persons acting in a similar capacity or by senior management of the issuer who believe that confirmation of the decision by the board of directors or any other persons acting in a similar capacity is probable.

- A company must file a report with securities authorities after completing a significant acquisition, providing some details of the acquisition.
- Proxies and information circulars must usually be filed to allow a shareholder to appoint a person or company to act on their behalf at a shareholder meeting.
- Information circulars prepared for an annual meeting of shareholders must also include detailed disclosure about the compensation paid to certain executive officers and directors in connection with their office or employment.
- If a reporting issuer has outstanding restricted securities, or securities convertible into or exchangeable for restricted securities, it must provide certain specified disclosure about those securities.
- Companies may be required to file copies of all material contracts entered into within the last financial year. Timing of such disclosures varies among legislative areas.

Continuous Reporting

The continuous disclosure requirements of securities regulators fall somewhat short of the idea of continuous reporting which has often been explored in the accounting literature.[2]

Continuous reporting is based on recognizing that the idea of periodic reporting is obsolete. Ideally it would involve an ability of companies to report on a real time basis 24/7—not just to report but to report comprehensive and properly constructed accounting reports. Such reporting would involve the ability to stream current transactions, calculate accruals and prepaids, make estimates and address valuations and judgments.

The time has come to say goodbye to quarterly reporting and quarterly earnings guidance. And not just for the usual reasons cited such as short-termism. In this day and age of "real-time everything," a quarterly reporting cadence is antiquated, pointless and unacceptable.[3]

One of the arguments against quarterly reporting is that it requires investors to wait for three months for their reports, which is an unreasonable length of time in the current age of instant information. Another argument is derived from the practice of companies issuing earnings estimates to make up for the lag until the next reports become available. The argument is that "Earnings forecasts foster bad behaviors, compelling short-term manipulations to make good on the estimate at period-end, irrespective of the impact on long-term shareholder value."[4] There is some merit in this argument as any auditor can confirm.

A strict application of continuous reporting can be achieved through a corporate website. As reports become available, they can be shown in the investor relations section of the website. However, making them available and current on a continuous basis requires that the accounting systems enable the flow of all data into a central system that accumulates it in financial statement form. It also requires that the appropriate adjusting entries must be able to be entered on a continuing basis—a process that has been referred to as a continuous close.

There has been "a shift among many midsize and larger enterprises to assist continuous accounting, using automated financial and accounting software to reconcile accounts, match transactions, and address variances on a daily basis."[5] Such continuous closing can be done with the right systems but relatively few companies have implemented such systems to date. For public companies, it also raises the question of continuous auditing, a subject of research prominently carried out at Rutgers University under the direction of Miklos Vasarhelyi, Director of the Rutgers Accounting Research Center and Continuous Auditing and Reporting Lab.

Other Regulatory Reports

Regulatory reports are numerous and, in certain industries, punitive. We have already mentioned the 10-Q and 10-K forms required by the SEC of companies listed in the United States. There are many more just within the SEC requirements, including among others, Registration Statements, Proxy Statements, and various schedules about ownership and changes in ownership.

In addition to the SEC, companies in the financial industry may have to file reports with the Federal Reserve Board (FRB) and/or the Federal Deposit Insurance Corporation (FDIC) and with various banking regulators in Canada, such as the CDIC (Canada Deposit Insurance Corporation) and OSFI (The Office of the Superintendent of Financial Institutions). All companies need to file numerous reports, including tax returns, with the Internal Revenue Agency (IRA) in the United States, the CRA in Canada and the HM Revenue and Customs (HMRC) in the UK. Moreover, various states and provinces have their own regulatory requirements.

The plethora of filing requirements, often involving much duplication, has given rise to complaints about red tape and regulatory overload and has led to suggested remedies such as coordinated or shared filing systems and the use of new technologies such as XBRL (Extensible Business Reporting Language).

XBRL is currently required by the SEC, HMRC, and Companies House as well as most of the major regulators around the world and can help with duplicate filings. This is because XBRL can be read by any recipient regardless of the system they are using, therefore eliminating the need to structure the data differently for each separate filing.

While XBRL has been widely adopted around the world, there have been few cases of it being used effectively to address regulatory overload. One exception might be in the UK, where the HMRC and Companies House entered into an agreement to jointly develop a filing system using XBRL where the filings would be shared with both agencies, thus eliminating one filing for the companies.

News Releases

Companies are obligated to provide timely notice of major events to stakeholders. Most regulators have requirements that all stakeholders be notified at the same time so that particular individual investors do not gain unfair advantages by having information that others do not have. New releases on a corporate website generally satisfy these requirements as do notices through social media such as Twitter. Most jurisdictions have released guidance on these matters.

Financial Reporting includes a broad range of reports provided by the company at the end of the year and also during the year. The reports are diverse and are issued in different forms and are available through different means. Most of them in one way or another end up being available on the Internet, either in the company's IR section of its website, in its website generally, or in the website of the regulators, such as the SEC, Companies House, or the OSC. Some are available through social media, such as Twitter or YouTube and to a lesser extent through Facebook and LinkedIn. When we discuss reporting on the Internet, all of these vehicles are relevant.

The Growing Volume of Information

While the components of corporate reporting have increased in numbers, they have also increased in volume. In recent years, annual reports of companies have grown from documents of perhaps twenty or thirty pages to hundreds of pages. For example, HSBC, the British Bank, recently published its 2019 annual report reaching nearly 600 pages while Barclays produced a document for that year that was 444 pages long. Numerous companies have reports of 200 pages or more. Moreover, they contain a good deal of information on complex economic issues, as well as very complex accounting issues, that strain the abilities of most readers not well trained in economics and accounting to understand them, and even of some who are.

The increased volume has been caused by the inclusion of much more narrative information than used to be the case. That in turn has been caused by

1. the growing complexity of business organizations;
2. a desire by stakeholders to make management more accountable;
3. increasing role of regulators dedicated to protecting stakeholders and the public in general; and
4. the growing body of corporate legislation and jurisprudence.

An example of this growth can be found in the financial statements, where, for example, the notes to the statements have compounded greatly in an attempt to explain the application of complex accounting standards, such as accounting for financial instruments, cryptocurrencies, and disclosure of forward-looking information. And the MD&A documents are now larger than the whole annual report used to be.

This growth in the volume of information reported by companies has led to a case of information overload, which can reduce the effectiveness of the reporting, since investors need to wade through a lot more information in order to find what they need. Use of the Internet can help with information overload because of the drill-down capability made possible through the use of hyperlinks. For example, a complicated income statement can be placed on the website, perhaps even in condensed form, with links to more detailed information, including breakdowns of income and expense items, and links to related information on the MD&A and other reports. This is a major advantage of the Internet, although many companies do not take advantage of it because they often present their statements in PDF form, which does permit hyperlinks but does not render them easy to use. More on this later.

CHAPTER 2

Stakeholder Needs

The original need for corporate financial reporting arose because of the division between ownership and management. Such reporting was crucial to enable the owners to keep abreast of the financial condition of their companies. With the creation of joint stock companies, investors relied heavily on reporting to evaluate their investments.

This elementary situation evolved quickly with bankers and other lenders demanding comprehensive financial reports and governments developing tax systems that require some form of reporting. The types of stakeholders gradually expanded as companies grew and became more important to their communities, regions, and countries. People also came to realize their impact was beyond financial, and included social and environmental matters, but the corporate response to these issues has been much slower.

With these various needs developing, the concept of general-purpose reporting evolved, as an attempt to satisfy most of the needs of the stakeholders as a group without necessitating the companies to report separately to each of them. This system has worked quite well for several decades, although separate reporting has existed, particularly in the case of reporting to governments and regulators, who often require supplementary reports.

In order for general-purpose reporting to satisfy user needs most effectively, standards boards have had to set out rules in the form of generally accepted accounting principles. Most of the standards-setting bodies started with the professional accounting bodies in individual countries, such as the American Institute of Certified Public Accountants (AICPA), Canadian Institute of Chartered Accountants (CICA), and the Institute of Chartered Accountants of England and Wales (ICAEW), but then evolved into independent organizations such as the Financial Accounting Standards Board (FASB) in the United States, the Accounting Standards

Board (ASB) in Canada, and the International Accounting Standards Board (IASB) internationally. Along with the individual standards on particular accounting issues, these bodies have set out objectives of general-purpose financial reporting that are roughly consistent around the world. The objectives are focused on how to best meet the needs of the stakeholders.

Objectives of Financial Reporting

According to the conceptual framework for financial reporting, "The objective of general-purpose financial reporting is to provide financial information about the reporting entity that is useful to existing and potential investors, lenders and other creditors in making decisions relating to providing resources to the entity. Those decisions involve:

a. buying, selling, or holding equity and debt instruments;
b. providing or settling loans and other forms of credit; or
c. exercising rights to vote on, or otherwise influence, management's actions that affect the use of the entity's economic resources."[1]

The conceptual framework goes on to set out the qualitative characteristics of financial information. It explicitly notes that the characteristics apply to all financial information, including the financial statements and other information.

First, the Framework begins with the fundamental characteristics relevance and faithful representation (Figure 2.1).

Relevance

Relevant information is defined as that which is capable of making a difference in stakeholder decisions. In order to be relevant, information must have predictive and/or confirmatory value.

Financial information need not be projections or forecasts in order to have predictive value. Rather it just needs to be useful as input into the processes that users follow in order to predict outcomes. For example, an income statement can have predictive value even though it deals with

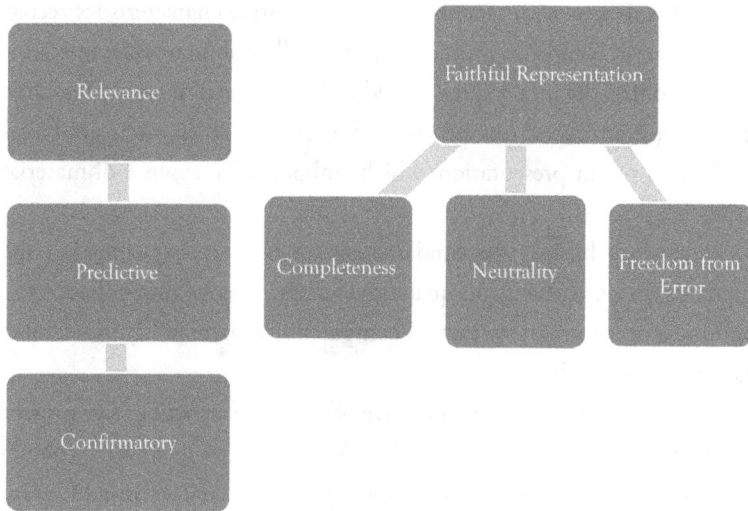

Figure 2.1 Qualitative characteristics

a past period because it can be used in comparison with other periods to develop trend analyses that provide pertinent information about the future.

Much research effort has been expended on the question of whether annual reports are revelatory or confirmatory. The consensus emerging out of this research was that they tend to be confirmatory rather than revelatory. In other words, they tend to confirm existing information rather than reveal new information. Much of the reason for this is because timely information, such as news releases and interim reports, is released before the annual reports, and indeed in many cases is required by the regulators to be released on a timely basis. Websites substantially improve on the timeliness factor, since documents don't need to be printed and mailed.

Faithful Representation

To have faithful representation, information must accurately reflect the substance of the underlying economic events being represented. Faithful representation includes three characteristics: completeness, neutrality, and freedom from error. Completeness means all material facts are included. Neutrality is freedom from bias. Freedom from error is self-explanatory but the FASB and IASB statements on qualitative characteristics recognize that perfect freedom from error is generally not attainable; instead it is expected that the information would be free of material error. Standards of assurance are based on the same idea, and audit opinions are based on the idea of fair presentation, which embodies the absence of material error.

Having established the fundamental qualitative characteristics, the standards go on to focus on qualitative characteristics that enhance the usefulness of information, that is, comparability, verifiability, timeliness, and understandability.

As mentioned earlier, the objective of financial reporting is to present information that is useful in making decisions. The qualitative characteristics simply provide an understanding of the characteristics of useful information. The main purpose of discussing the qualitative characteristics in this book is to be able to indicate the impact of the Internet on those characteristics. Does it make the information more useful? Why or why not? We will pick up this line of thought later in this and the next chapter. In the meantime, we need to focus on the various types of stakeholders and their needs. (Figure 2.2)

Investors, including prospective investors, purchase common and preferred shares in companies, debentures, and various other financial instruments that a company might offer. Their needs vary according to the types of financial instrument they purchase. Overall, they need to decide whether to buy, sell, hold, or redeem their investments.

All investors are interested in the strength of the financial position of the company and its recent earnings. They also are interested in the prospects of the company for future earnings. Common shareholders have a special interest in the earnings, since their success or failure is directly dependent on the past and prospective earnings of the company.

Public company shareholders have a wider range of interests because their investments are listed on a stock exchange. Because the instruments on stock exchanges are usually common shares, they have an interest in earnings. However, their investments are also subject to the vagaries of the stock market, which vary according to numerous events that might have an effect on the company, such as those of a political or environmental nature, economic conditions, rumours, and so on.

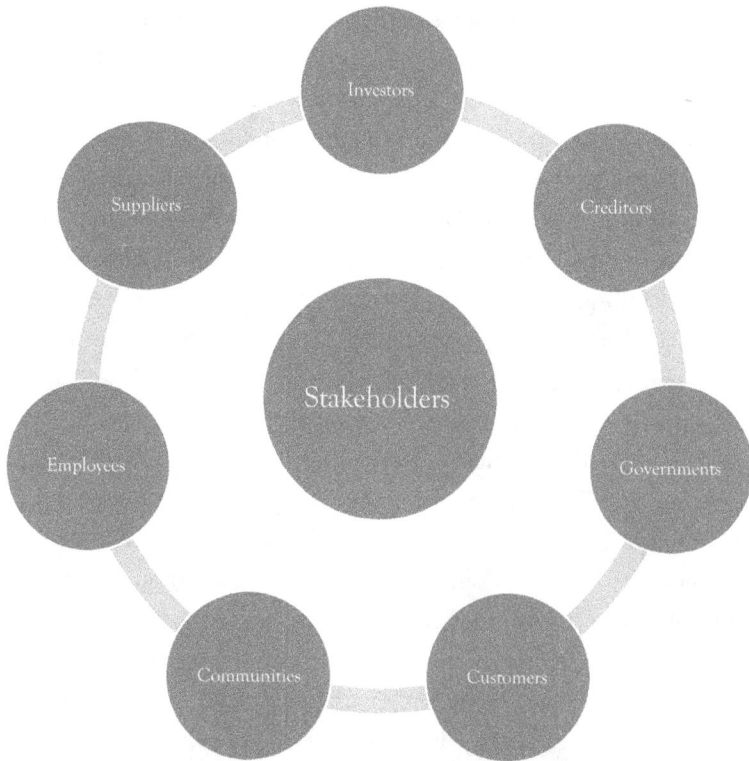

Figure 2.2 Stakeholders

Financial reporting to public company shareholders is a complex web of needs, conventions, regulations, and changing times. We have introduced the idea of their needs, which tend to change over time, for example, with changing social mores, changing ways of doing business, and changing technologies, corporate structures, and financial instruments in which to invest. Financial reporting, on the other hand, has been bound by convention since the beginning. There have been conventions about the style of reporting, for example, the focus on earnings, financial position, and changes in financial position. Indeed, the myriad of rules (Generally Accepted Accounting Principles [GAAP]) around how to calculate and present the various components of these reports, are themselves built on convention, such as the cost principle, lower of cost and market, conservatism, and matching revenues and expenses.

Conventions tend to change slowly, and can therefore get out of tune with the times—and with investor needs. On the other hand, they add a high degree of much needed stability to the reporting process.

Creditors include trade creditors, mortgage holders, commercial lenders, bond holders, banks, basically anyone to whom the company owes money. Most of them have their own requirements for reporting, which sometimes include regular financial statements but more often include additional information, such as metrics in which they are interested or additional detail about particular items. They often prescribe the form of reports they require.

Governments are, of course, major stakeholders of companies large and small. Certainly, they are major users of financial statements and a myriad of other reports. They require reporting by companies for purposes of taxation, whether it be income taxes, consumption taxes, sales taxes, employee taxes, property taxes, or business taxes. The reporting varies, with reporting for income tax purposes generally being the most sophisticated and bearing the strongest resemblance to reporting to shareholders.

Customers become dependent on the company for their supplies, especially if they are running a business as well. Quite often, the customers share in supply chain systems and get a good deal of information from those systems, although they vary in effectiveness as information sources. Accordingly, the customers are interested in the financial strength of the company as well as its plans for developing and maintaining products.

Communities include local, regional, and national levels. Sometimes the interests of the different levels of community coincide. Often, they don't. A major concern of local communities is the extent to which the company provides jobs. Another is the effect of the company on the local environment. If a company pollutes the water or the air, then it will be usually looked upon with disfavor. So, the communities are concerned not only about the financial strength of the companies, but also the environmental impact of the companies. Environmental reporting is critical to communities.

Employees, of course, are concerned about their jobs, their rate of pay, their prospect for advancement, and working conditions. They need information about the financial condition of the company, its earnings, and its strategic plans for the future.

Suppliers sell to a company, and wish to maintain a profitable business. They are also part of the supply chain. Therefore, they are interested in the financial strength of the company as well as its plans for developing and maintaining products.

Financial analysts are another group of users that is important to several of these other user groups, including especially investors, creditors, and governments. Analysts play a major role in the use and interpretation of corporate reporting. They do detailed analysis and modelling in order to increase understanding of the financial results and identify trends from the past and for the future. Their reports are announced in various publications, and directly affect stock market movements.

It is generally accepted that corporate reports do not in themselves provide enough information to meet the needs of the analysts. That is why companies typically hold analyst meetings to provide the analysts with more in-depth information and often provide additional information to them on request, although the information they do provide must also be available to others under the securities laws. Financial analysts are one of the most important components of the reporting supply chain. The Web presents a major opportunity to present information that will make the job of the analysts easier. The navigability of websites through Web links and menu systems make it easier to gather information than from print-based documents. Also, websites offer an opportunity to present data in forms that can be used for analysis. Data presented in old-fashioned print reports is meant just to be read. Users who want to do serious analysis need to download the data and enter it into their own analytical tools or spreadsheets such as Excel. An often-repeated theme in this book is that the presentation of data in the form of PDF files is very much a missed opportunity because those data cannot be used directly for analysis, whereas data presented in spreadsheets or other means can be used directly.

Environmental, social, and governance (ESG) reporting by corporations was once of interest to a small group of investors and others. Now, with the growing interest in environmental concerns, ESG has become a major area of interest. Companies have long had to report to their investors, but according to Chris Ruggeri, national managing principal at Deloitte, in reporting on Deloitte's 2019 CEO survey, "CFOs and

IROs have a growing list of stakeholders beyond Wall Street: customers, employees, vendors, regulators, philanthropists, social responsibility monitors and others who want to know how their company's strategy and financial performance are benefiting their community and the world at large."[2]

According to a report from Morgan Stanley, the number of S&P 500 companies publishing some form of ESG disclosure increased from 20 percent in 2011 to 86 percent in 2018, a massive change for companies. And stakeholders are making use of the information by broadening the range of metrics used in evaluating corporate performance. This is consistent with the recent statement of the Business Roundtable on the purpose of a corporation, which can be found on its website.[3] It broadens the purpose of companies well beyond simply making money, although that is of course still central and very important, but does include the idea of supporting the communities in which they work, respecting the people in their communities and protecting the environment by embracing sustainable practices across their businesses.

To further complicate the needs of stakeholders, the nature of business has changed greatly over the past few decades. Whereas once the assets of a business consisted of such things as buildings, vehicles, inventories, receivables, and other tangibles, now many businesses are service-oriented and depend more heavily on the skills of their people. They also depend heavily on their relationships with customers and others and the existence of a reliable flow of income. Not all of this is new, but there is a compounding effect in that businesses are dependent more than ever on non-tangible assets as opposed to tangibles. Traditional corporate reporting focuses on reporting tangibles and does very little of reporting on intangibles. Any reporting there of intangible assets is done in narrative form, with little attempt to place a monetary value on them.

Now in the twenty-first century, corporate reporting has evolved to include reporting on the Internet. That's a big change in media and as Marshall McLuhan used to say, "The Medium is the Message."

That is an important concept for corporate reporting on the Internet. The very fact that reporting is presented on the Internet has led to a gradual increase in the use of multimedia, such as video and interactive graphics in IR websites.

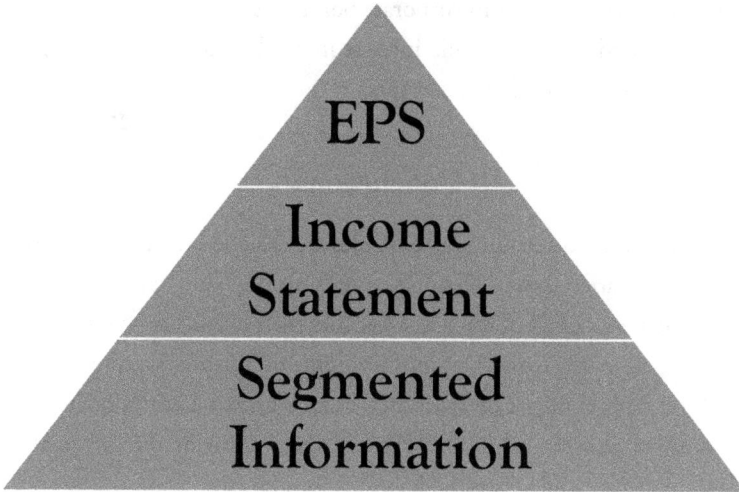

EPS

Income Statement

Segmented Information

Figure 2.3 Sample of pyramid disclosure

Another aspect of the Internet that impacts on corporate reporting is the fact that it is a medium that can accommodate vast quantities of data, unlike traditional print media, so the IR sites have been including more presentations of data, a trend just beginning and explored further in Chapter 4.

Finally, the Internet is useful for presenting information that is linked to other information. That opens up the door for disclosures that are structured like a pyramid, with highly summarized information at the top, perhaps on an investor relations website page with links to more detailed information such as components of the information, which is in turn linked to further detail about those components. This can proceed all the way to detailed data to support any of the components, although this degree of depth is rarely presented by companies, particularly in public disclosures. Along the way, there can be links to the Management, Discussion and Analysis and other documents to provide more in-depth information about a particular item of information.

The power of the Web to present information detail in the depth needed by stakeholders cannot be overestimated. Each of the stakeholder types is interested in information in different degrees of detail. For example, financial analysts are noted for asking for (demanding?) more detailed information about many items of disclosure. At the other end of the spectrum, an investor in corporate bonds has just a general interest in operations, and a more specific interest in the liquidity of the company and its ability to meet debt covenants.

Conclusions

Generally accepted accounting principles are designed to satisfy the needs of as wide a variety of stakeholders as possible, but they cannot fully satisfy all the needs of all of the users, because their needs vary considerably. At least some of the expansion in the volume of information presented in corporate reports might be attributed to an effort to accommodate these needs. It has also moved to the Web in order to provide the information in a more timely and accessible form.

The attributes of the Web, particularly the ability to link pieces of information. thus making separately presented items of information all part of the same reading experience, make it a very powerful tool. The pyramid style of reporting information enables users to drill down to the levels of information they need for their purposes.

Most of the elements of the qualitative characteristics could be enhanced through the use of the Web. Because of the ability to link information, relevant information can more easily be presented in context and in readily available fashion. As mentioned, faithful representation includes three characteristics—completeness, neutrality, and freedom from error. Information can be presented more completely, again, because of the ability to link the information needed to make it complete. Neutrality and freedom from error are perhaps not so affected.

CHAPTER 3

Contemporary Corporate Websites

While most companies today have websites, they serve very different purposes from company to company. For some companies that rely on online sales, like Amazon, Apple, and Dell, their website is their lifeblood. All or a majority of their business is conducted through those sites. For companies that sell services, like banks, the website offers information about their products and also offers some of their services, like online banking, through their website. Other service companies like the big accounting firms use their websites to provide information about their areas of interest. For all companies, public relations is an important part of their public image, so most include a variety of information about a company that is likely to be of interest to prospective customers and the general public and sets out information about the business, its products, locations, activities, and generally its contributions to society.

E-commerce takes several forms ranging from sale of goods and services to banking services. With the advent of the COVID-19 pandemic in 2020, the e-commerce element of websites is growing quickly as people do more of their shopping online.

Corporate websites serve several purposes for companies in addition to e-commerce and marketing. Significant among these purposes is that of investor relations. The Investor Relations section in a website generally includes financial reporting and other items of interest to investors. ESG reporting often appears in the Investor Relations section as well.

Every year, *IR Magazine*[1] runs awards programs focusing on investor relations websites, in various countries, including the United States, UK, Canada, Hong Kong, and Singapore. One of the judges listed their key recommendations to companies aspiring to produce a great IR website as follows:

1. Ensure your results archive is quick and easy to find.
2. Include transcripts and Excel financials in your results section.
3. Add short video commentaries to quarterly results.
4. Make the most of the Web's interactive potential.
5. Give plenty of details about your IR team.
6. Provide an overview of the company.
7. Give individual shareholders a warm welcome.
8. Pack your PDF reports with hyperlinks.

These recommendations are consistent with those of other IR professionals. Making the site and the key information in it, such as financial results, easy to find seems an obvious point, but it is surprising how many companies do not make an effort to achieve this simple characteristic. The format of the information is also important, as that can make the information easy to use. For example, financials set out in Excel form can be downloaded and analyzed or reformatted for analytical purposes. The uses of videos and interactive graphics are good alternatives to textual communication, enhancing the value of the information and adding interest.

Examples of top-rated IR websites from the US Awards of 2019 include:

1. Zurich: https://zurich.com/investor-relations (Figure 3.1)

The Zurich website exhibits a clean design with easy and effective navigation. It begins with a "proposition to investors," which outlines key features of the company from an investor standpoint. That is an equivalent of a section that other companies often feature titled "Why invest?" It gives an investor or prospective investor high level reasons why they should invest in the company. In Zurich's case, the features are a balanced and diverse global business, sound capital levels, a consistent and conservatively managed balance sheet, and consistent growth with scope to enhance returns through capital re-deployment.

The site then contains the company's annual report in its entirety and provides excellent additional information on the financial results. There is a section on news and upcoming events, such as the next annual meeting. There is a separate section devoted to the concerns of shareholders.

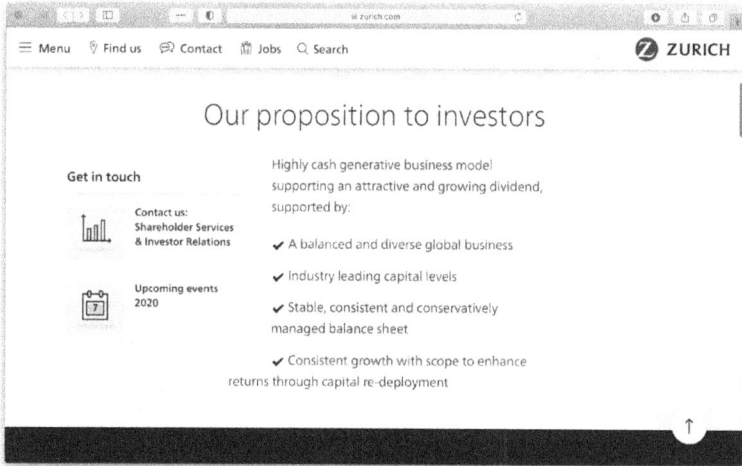

Figure 3.1 Zurich investor proposition

Overall, the Zurich site is attractive and provides a vast array of useful information for shareholders and other investors. A separate section set apart from the IR Section provides a sustainability report on environmental concerns.

2. AXA - https://axa.com/en/investor (Figure 3.2)

The AXA IR Site contains all the information mentioned in the Zurich site and is also presented in an attractive and useful way. An additional feature of the site is directed to shareholders, where they can compute

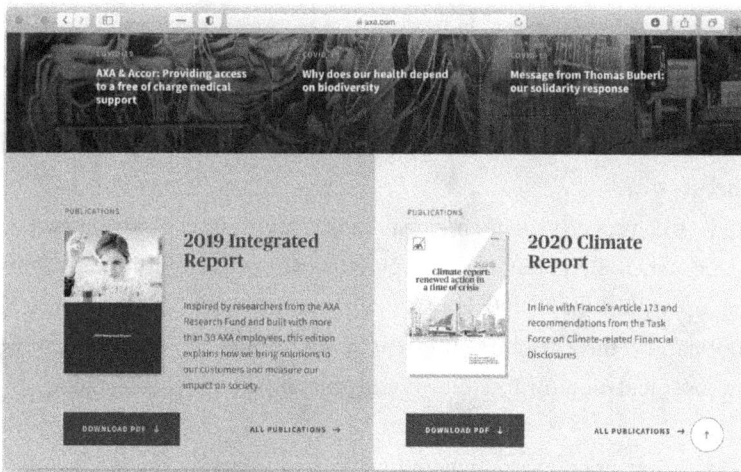

Figure 3.2 AXA Reports

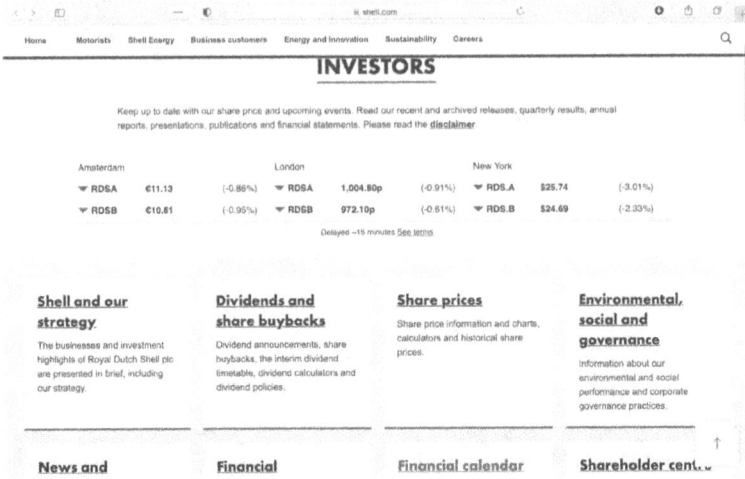

Figure 3.3 Shell investor page

their own return on investment. Such interactivity is a growing feature of good IR websites.

The site also offers an Integrated Report for download. These will be discussed in a later chapter, but in general an integrated report is one that integrates the financial and ESG reports into a single report, rather than leaving them in two or three separate reports.

  3. Shell: https://shell.com/investors.html (Figure 3.3)

Shell of course has a different story to tell than the other companies mentioned so far, since it is a major oil player rather than an insurance company. Accordingly, the Shell site presents up front a broad range of issues, including a separate environmental, social, and governmental (ESG) report, information on strategy, and of course financial reports and calendar, share price calculators, dividend reports and news reports.

  4. BP: https://bp.com/en/global/corporate/investors.html (Figure 3.4)

Like Shell, BP places a high importance on sustainability and presents a report within the IR Section. Also, in addition to the normal financial information, there is quite an extensive set of investor tools for making various calculations of interest to individual investors. These include:

  a. Share price chart—where investors can obtain comparative data on BP share prices over recent periods of up to a year.

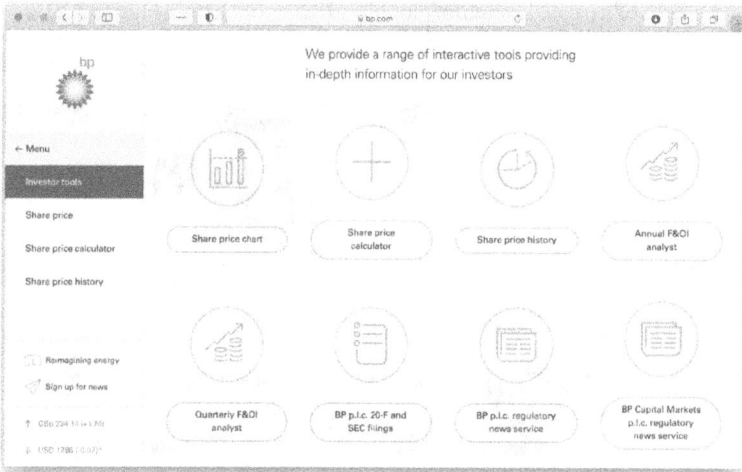

Figure 3.4 BP investor page

b. Share price calculator—where investors can calculate changes in the value of their shareholdings over recent periods.

c. Share price history—showing the history of BP share prices on various exchanges.

d. Annual F&OI analyst—which offers summarized annual operating data and also includes interactive tools to aid in analysis of the numbers.

e. Quarterly Financial & Operating Information analyst—which offers summarized quarterly operating data and also includes interactive tools to aid in analysis of the numbers.

f. BP p.l.c. 20-F and SEC filings—This section includes downloadable copies of 20-F reports as far back as 1981 in Word, Excel, PDF, and XBRL formats.

g. BP p.l.c. regulatory news service—which transmits regulatory and non-regulatory information published by companies and organizations allowing them to comply with local market transparency legislation.

h. BP Capital Markets p.l.c. regulatory news service—Similar to the preceding item.

Like the others, the BP site is very well designed and offers clear and easy navigation. The site makes good use of webcasts, more so than many other sites.

5. BASF: https://basf.com/global/en/investors.html (Figure 3.5)

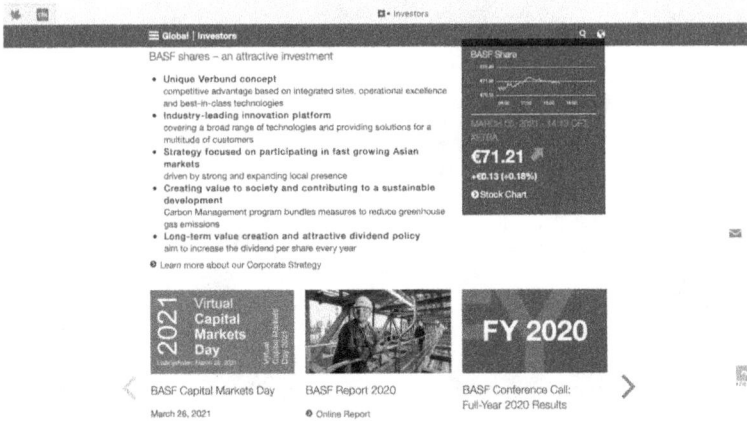

Figure 3.5 BASF Screen capture

BASF is the second largest chemical producer in the world. The BASF Group operates in more than 80 countries and 390 other production sites in Europe, Asia, Australia, the Americas, and Africa. Again, its IR site places a strong emphasis on environmental concerns with a section on sustainability and green investments. The section on sustainability addresses their goals, strategies, plans for the future, and recent news regarding sustainability. There is also a section on credit analysts, which includes information on the company's experience with rating agencies along with details of their bond debt and strategy regarding debt.

6. Daimler: https:// daimler.com/investors/ (Figure 3.6)

This producer of luxury automobiles has a website to match the quality of its product. Some of the more important sections of the IR section of the report include:

1. Share—shows comparative data, including graphs of Daimler share price trends.
2. Reports and News—includes annual and interim reports and other reports along with news items about and related to the company.
3. Refinancing—includes information on the corporate financial management, debt agency ratings, bonds, green finance, and other information.

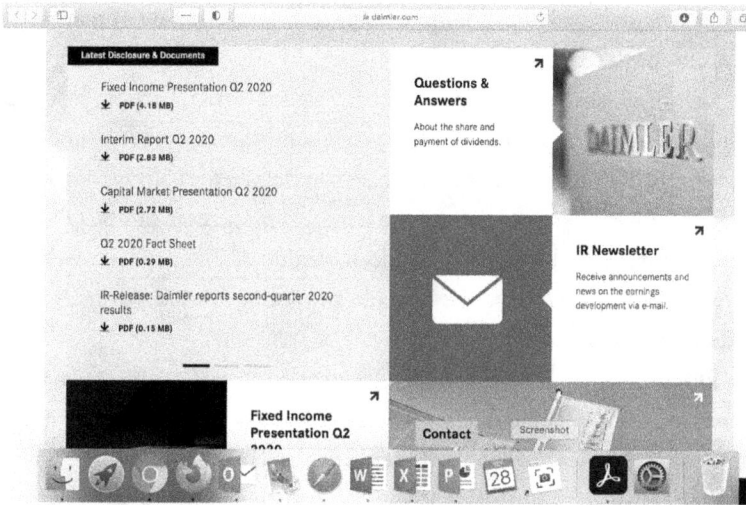

Figure 3.6 Daimler disclosure documents

4. Key figures—presents various key performance indicators in tabular form, PDFs, and graphs.
5. Events—includes key events on the investor calendar.
6. About Us—summarizes information about Daimler, its history, and organization.
7. Services—focuses on investor relations services and includes a media center with various reports, presentations, and videos.

There is also a large separate section outside the investor relations section on ESG matters. Downsides of the Daimler site are that, as with most companies to date, the ESG section is not integrated with the investor relations section. Also many of the data reports are presented in PDF form, which as mentioned elsewhere does not facilitate analysis.

Distinguishing Marketing and Financial Information Content

One of the difficulties of Internet reporting is distinguishing between marketing content and true fact-based financial reporting. That's not to say it's all difficult. For example, audited financial statements are clearly part of the financial reporting while information about the company generally and its products are more likely to be in the nature of marketing or promotional content.

Use of a clearly marked Investor Relations (IR) Section helps in distinguishing the information. Even then, though, the boundaries between the IR information and other materials are not always apparent. The use of weblinks complicates the issue, since the user can be taken to a place outside the IR section or indeed outside of the corporate website. Some, but not all, companies provide a warning for users when a link takes them outside the home website.

Distinguishing between an ESG report and marketing information can be much more difficult. That's because more of the information in the ESG report is soft and although there are standards, such as those issued by the Global Reporting Initiative (GRI), such standards, while widely accepted, are not mandatory.

Responsibilities of Participants

Distinguishing the nature of the information helps the investors to determine how useful the information is likely to be in making investment related decisions. Determining who has the responsibility for the accuracy of the information helps in assessing its accuracy.

Management is primarily responsible for all the information on a corporate website. However, if some of the information is audited or the auditor is associated with it in any way, management shares some of that responsibility with the auditors. So, it is important to know where the audited information ends and the unaudited information begins. That is not always readily apparent. For example, the audited financial statements might have schedules with them outlining some details of audited items. Normally, the auditors do not express an opinion on those schedules and in fact they are typically marked as unaudited, so they do not have direct responsibility for them. However, the schedules do contain information related to the financial statements and to the extent that misstatements might distort the financial statements, they might have responsibility. Also, the auditors have some basic responsibility for other information in an annual report outside of the financial statements. There has been some discussion as well, as to whether the auditors have a similar responsibility for other information in the website, although most auditors would argue that they cannot possibly read the corporate website to see if there are any inconsistencies with the audited financial statements. Some ambiguity in this matter will continue until clearer standards and guidance are released.

Outsourcing

A study carried out by Pendley and Rai in 2008 explored the way firms use the Internet for financial reporting, given the advancements in Internet technologies that have altered the methods used to design and deploy websites. They examined the websites of a sample of U.S. companies during the period 2006–2007 and did find a major structural change in the method used to deliver online financial reports. This change involved the increased use of third-party outsourcing services in the delivery of online financial information. Pendley and Rai concluded that

> Almost 59 per cent of firms engage in some form of outsourcing and nearly 41 per cent completely outsource their financial reporting site. Although the increased use of outsourcing may be a rational and expected way to provide online accounting data, outsourcing poses many unexplored ramifications for the accounting profession, including the nature and quality of the data, regulation of online financial data and the role of emerging technologies, such as XBRL, for business arrangements.[2]

Most of these ramifications relate to the fact that management remains responsible for the financial reporting, even when it is outsourced, and therefore has a responsibility to ensure that the final reports on the website are the same as the actual authorized reports. This is particularly complex in the case of XBRL disclosures, which is explored further in Chapter 5.

Outsourcing refers to the use of outside consultants that provide and maintain an investor relations (IR) website for a company. Pendley and Rai distinguished between sites that were fully outsourced and those that were partially outsourced: (i) "An investor relations website is considered fully outsourced if it is hosted and maintained by an outside investor relations services firm."[3] and (ii) "A partially outsourced site exhibits some of the characteristics of a fully outsourced site, such as certain (but not all) accounting reports obtained from a third-party database or Webcast files linked to a consulting service's media library. However, it is uncertain whether the investor relations site is hosted by an investor relations consulting firm."[4]

Advantages of Internet Financial Reporting

Timeliness. Use of the Internet makes it possible to improve the timeliness of financial reporting. The time required to print and mail or otherwise distribute the reports is eliminated. Reports can be made available within minutes of being prepared.

Availability. In the earlier days of the Internet, there were concerns about the use of the Internet for financial reporting because it was felt that many people did not have access to the Internet. Twenty years ago, smartphones did not exist, Internet speeds were slow, and Internet access was not widespread. But that quickly changed and now virtually everyone has Internet access, the exceptions being in some rural communities with sparse populations. That means that if a company publishes its annual report on its website, most of those people can quickly gain access to it. People in general, therefore, have much better access to financial reports than they did when they had to be on a mailing list with the company or had to get the reports from their banker or stockbroker.

Interactivity. With the Internet, reports can be downloaded and then combined with other information that enhances their understanding, such as industry data, demographic data, and so on. Moreover, the information in the reports can be manipulated and analyzed in spreadsheets or other analytical tools provided it is in a form that makes this possible. PDF files generally make such analysis difficult, while HTML, XBRL, and spreadsheet data can more easily be used in this manner.

Hyperlinking. The use of hyperlinks is a major advantage of using the Internet. It means that relevant information to add to the understanding of a fact can be quickly identified and accessed. A good example of this is the use of footnotes to the financial statements. The references to the relevant footnotes usually included on the face of the financial statements can be hyperlinked to the notes, enabling readers to simply click the link and read the note. This is a major improvement in the ability of users to understand the statements.

Similarly, the items in the financial statements can be linked to the relevant items in the MD&A, to enhance understanding of those items. *Multimedia.* The use of multimedia in websites can significantly aid in the understanding of financial reports and often is used effectively. This would include videos of presentations, graphics, and photos. Videos and graphics are particularly effective.

Qualitative characteristics. The discussion of qualitative characteristics above pointed to timeliness, which has already been discussed in this section. Relevance is also improved in the sense that it is easier to show relevant information through weblinks as well as the advantage of not being bound by the constraints of conventional paginated information. For example, number of pages on a website is not as big a problem as with printed material.

Disadvantages of Internet Financial Reporting

Availability of Internet. As mentioned above, availability of the Internet was once a major prohibitive factor, but is not so much of a problem now since Internet services have improved. However, lack of availability still exists for a minority of the population, especially in rural areas, and printed materials still need to be made available to them.

Technological Prowess

There are also people who simply do not have much ability in using technology, even though they might have it available. For them, Internet disclosure may not help very much. Also, if the information can be downloaded, it increases the possibility of errors being introduced. Overall, however, the vast majority of people use the Internet daily and are very accustomed to using websites. Moreover, the technology is always improving to make the use of websites easier.

Conclusions

Overall it is clear that financial reporting on the Internet is a very positive development in the world of reporting to stakeholders and investor relations. It makes reporting more available and more timely to interested parties. It also offers up opportunities to present the information in ways that will have a greater appeal to people. The availability of popular devices such as smartphones has also led to expectations that information will be available on the Internet and can be read on those devices. There is no longer a valid basis for debate as to whether corporate reporting should be presented on the Internet or on paper. The Internet has won quite decisively.

CHAPTER 4

The Movement to Data

Data has become big in recent years, both in terms of volume and importance, and "Big Data" has become one of the latest "buzz words." But it is real, and it and all data have become an important element of the latest business decision making, both for strategic and operational purposes.

Big data is often defined in terms of volume, velocity, and variety. "Volume refers to the amount of data generated through websites, portals and online applications … Facebook has 2 billion users, Youtube 1 billion users, Twitter 350 million users and Instagram 700 million users."[1] They generate an incredible volume of data.

> Velocity refers to the speed with which data are being generated. Staying with our social media example, every day 900 million photos are uploaded on Facebook, 500 million tweets are posted on Twitter, 0.4 million hours of video are uploaded on Youtube and 3.5 billion searches are performed in Google.[2]

On May 21, 2018, *Forbes* reported that "There are 2.5 quintillion bytes of data created each day at our current pace … Over the last two years alone 90 percent of the data in the world was generated."[3] Since then, the amount of data has continued to grow.

Within businesses, according to a 2019 survey from Matillion and IDG, "Optimizing Business Analytics by Transforming Data in the Cloud," data volumes are growing at an average of 63 percent per month, with 12 percent of organizations reporting over 100 percent growth every month. According to a survey by IDC, in 2018 alone, storage suppliers added more than 700 exabytes of storage capacity to keep up with growing data volumes.[4] One exabyte equals one quintillion bytes.

"Enterprises are struggling to keep pace. With a daily average of 2.5 quintillion bytes of data created, business users and executive teams are barely able to stay afloat in the growing amount of data incoming from IoT (Internet of Things) devices, Artificial Intelligence and Machine Learning technologies. This data growth change is only expected to increase, leaving companies grappling with how to manage it all in an efficient manner."[5]

"Variety in Big Data refers to all the structured and unstructured data that has the possibility of being generated either by humans or by machines."[6] Structured data is structured to various degrees and includes, for example, most database data, HTML and XBRL data, and pictures and videos. Examples of unstructured data are e-mails, texts, tweets, voicemails, and audio recordings.

Structured data comes in the form of data sets that have been digitized in such a way that they can be used by importing them into analytical tools that simply sort, categorize, and compare the information and then apply advanced analytics to develop historical trends, comparisons, projections, and various metrics relevant to the particular decisions to be made.

Unstructured data, on the other hand, as the name implies, is data that is not in a form that can be readily used by computer systems. Typically, for example, it includes data buried in text documents or other reports. To be useful, it needs to be scanned, extracted, and then converted into structured data—a process that can be very time consuming and can lead to serious inconsistencies if left in the hands of the individual users.

Companies, analysts, and data purveyors are spending millions to develop tools to capture and analyze big data. Business users often make use of the kinds of data generated by social media as mentioned above. However, they are also, perhaps even more, interested in data generated by business transactions. Most enterprise wide business systems include the ability to generate large amounts of data from the billions of transactions that take place. A prime example is found in Business Intelligence systems that are used to gather information about the transactions and the customers that initiate them. They typically gather as much information as they can, much beyond name and address and other personal information to include items purchased, time of day, browsing habits, method of payment, and other products of possible interest. Data on client characteristics such as age, gender, spending habits, and location might be collected and then used to develop metrics for marketing purposes or Key Performance Indicators (KPIs) for reporting purposes. This information can feed into marketing efforts, store organization, product offerings, timing of sales, and so on.

Although big data is a growing area, it is in many respects an emerging area for financial reporting, so good examples are relatively rare on current IR websites. However, interactive Analyst Centers of the type referred to above are ideal for displaying KPIs, which can then be used by analysts for understanding the company reporting them. Both of the example sites above contain KPIs that are somewhat similar to these and can be seen on their Analyst Centers. We can be sure that we will see much more of this in the future.

In the modern world, the big data phenomenon is changing the way people make decisions. Instead of drawing small samples of data for a decision, they use whole or very large populations of data. The effect is to reduce the elements of judgment and estimation, which bring in so many inconsistencies and errors. See also "Big Data and Corporate Reporting: Impacts and Paradoxes" by Khaldoon Al-Htaybat and Larissa von Alberti-Alhtaybat.[7]

The production of data in traditional text format is an obsolete relic of the age of print, designed for human reading—and useful to that degree—but not designed for serious analytics. In the world of investing, therefore, the idea of reading annual reports and then making investment decisions is similarly a relic of a bygone age. People are using analytical tools, such as spreadsheets and those on the websites of investment dealers and banks and online investing sites such as those offered by most large financial institutions, like BMO Investorline, J P Morgan Wealth Management, or Chase.com.

Most of the data from these institutions is structured data. But the existence of unstructured data, such as print-based reports and much of the data characterized as big data, is difficult to handle and adds to the cost of consuming the information. Unstructured data can be converted into structured data by presenting it in a form, such as spreadsheets, that can be used and analyzed by the users. It can also be converted through a process of tagging the data. This simply means that the data are enhanced by adding additional information—called metadata—and then feeding the data into analytical tools that, because they are now computer readable, can take it from there. An advantage of structured information is that standards can be set that help users cull through volumes of information and help them find meaningful information wherever it is. An example of standards for structured data can be found in eXtensible Business Reporting Language (XBRL) standards.

Fortunately, such data for investing purposes are available in the United States and several other countries through the use of XBRL. Unfortunately, most of the XBRL data is financial statement data, which was already partially structured, but there is very little XBRL data for unstructured data. This can be addressed, however, because tools like XBRL can be used on unstructured data, thus converting them to structured. Companies would do well to make greater use of this technique in presenting big data on their websites.

Traders and analytics specialists are placing greater emphasis on XBRL data, as they are totally structured, represent a population of most of the listed companies in the United States, and therefore provide a sound basis for making investment decisions based on all the facts.

As of 2018, the SEC adopted amendments that require companies to provide their financial statements in interactive XBRL by submitting them to the SEC *and* posting them on their corporate websites. Through this means and similar edicts issued by other regulators around the world, XBRL became a format used for the reporting of financial information on websites.

XBRL data had previously been required to be filed with the SEC and were reported on the SEC's EDGAR website starting in 2010, but this new rule enforced the idea of reporting the information on the corporate websites as well. In 2018, however, the SEC dropped the requirement to disclose the XBRL data on the corporate websites. Nevertheless, many companies still do disclose this information. The provision of financial statements and other data in various formats, additional to PDF, such as HTML, Excel, and XBRL is a characteristic of the best websites because it enables users to make use of the information in ways that are convenient and familiar to them. The reporting of information using XBRL is explored further in the next chapter.

Initially there were serious quality issues with the XBRL data filed with the SEC. Items were misclassified and tags misused. However, through studies of the data and additional instruction and training and improvements in the specifications for preparing the filings, the quality of the data has improved over more recent years, though quality issues remain.

Data-Driven Decision Making

The reliance of business managers on volumes of data in making decisions has been referred to as data-driven decision making. There is a strong desire in business to make use of the data available and thereby reduce the reliance on judgment, opinion, and pre-conceptions in order to be able to make stronger decisions. Whole industries have developed around this concept, not to mention numerous academic and other training programs.

Powerful information technology systems have made more and more data available to management and others. This includes information made available within a company through their day-to-day applications as well as data made available through various Business Information Systems. It also includes data made available by others in the industry, governments, and information on competitors and customers.

The huge volume of information has led to new and innovative ways to analyze the information. Many companies are currently involved in experimenting with different ways to use Artificial Intelligence (AI) in financial reporting. Since data-driven decision making has entered into the world of investment analysis, the use of AI to analyze data and produce usable metrics for reporting may well be reflected on corporate websites in the future.

Impact of Big Data on Financial Accounting

Big data is being incorporated into accounting systems. In addition to large amounts of numerical data, this includes data sources like text, video, and audio. In addition, big data may bring about substantial change to fair value accounting. Various accounting standards call for certain assets to be valued at fair value and this has a direct impact on the measurement of income. "Data service companies specializing in collecting and evaluating designated data from various sources could emerge, such that big data pertaining to the fair value of assets and liabilities can mitigate subjective assumptions in fair value estimates."[8]

Predictive analytics is already being used in financial accounting to mitigate the subjectivity in decisions being made.

Data-analytic thinking is increasingly being used for making investments decisions. Corporate websites are or should be a primary source for good data for those decisions. The rise of analytics means that corporate reporting needs to include more data suitable for analysis.

As stated in a recent study from New York University, "businesses increasingly are driven by data analytics, and there is great professional advantage in being able to interact competently with and within such businesses … having frameworks for organizing data-analytic thinking, not only will allow one to interact competently, but will help to envision opportunities for improving data-driven decision making or to see data-oriented competitive threats."[9] Corporate reporting on websites is the best and perhaps the only way to shape corporate reporting to the needs of investors who follow data-driven decision making.

Needs of Financial Analysts for Data

With the trend in recent years toward data-driven decision making, companies often look to financial analysts to help them make decisions based on data. The analysts play a critical role by examining data and providing actionable information on the profitability, solvency, stability, and liquidity of the company. Based on data provided by the analyst, the company also writes its own financial reports.

Corporate financial analysts operate every day with the company's goals and current financial situation in mind. They apply that focus to their work analyzing budgets, income statement forecasts, and other financial data. They collect and summarize data to build complex reports that clearly illustrate the company's financial status and any risks that may exist. They also establish financial benchmarks against which they measure company performance, and produce financial models to help decision makers determine how particular changes in behavior or market conditions could impact the business in the future.

Corporate financial analysts are called upon to keep a finger on the pulse of the business. While analyzing business performance, they often review and compare present data to past and projected performance, as well as the performance of competitors. Their recommendations also take into account industry and internal trends that suggest the future financial trajectory of the business. These findings are often published and result in the expectations that guide performance of the financial markets. When actual corporate results deviate from expectations, the prices are adjusted by market forces.

Data Visualization

The availability of vast amounts of data and the desire to make data-driven decisions have led to a greater use of data visualization, which is the graphical representation of data. Data visualization has been used for decades, with data being represented in the form of line charts, bar charts, pie charts, and area charts. Circles, balls, squares, and boxes are all used regularly.

Many new tools have evolved as well, with one of the most popular for accounting and finance professionals being Tableau and Alteryx. There are others, such as Izenda, Damo, Clicdata, Looker, and Yellowfin.

This graphic is from https://tableau.com/learn/articles/data-visualization (Figure 4.1). Various other presentations can be seen on that page, most of which are dynamic and interactive, which cannot be fully shown in a print book.

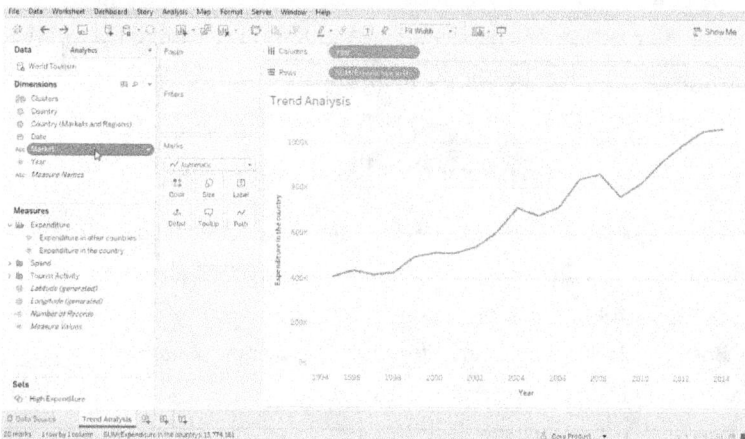

Figure 4.1 Trend analysis on website

The main point to remember about data visualization and corporate reporting on the Internet is that corporate reporting needs to recognize this is the way decisions are made and that decision makers are getting used to data visualization. Accordingly, there is a need to use data visualization on the websites. Most of the companies do use data visualization in some basic way; however, advanced, dynamic, interactive visualizations are relatively rare and represent a missed opportunity.

Data Disclosure in Current Websites

Big data has the potential to change accounting standards significantly. Many argue that current accounting standards are artifacts of an era subjected to high transmission costs and slow data collection speeds; however, such working conditions have become obsolete. To be relevant, accounting standards must focus on data rather than presentation. The U.S. academic John Peter Krahel and William R. Titera, a retired EY partner, proposed in 2015 that "accounting standards will have to deal with the content of the databases and allowable sets of extractions but not with the particular rules of account disclosure."[10] This is in part what XBRL was supposed to accomplish—provide all the content and context without limiting it to a specific presentation. Put another way, if we have standardized, trustworthy details, then any reports and rules to create reports are a happy by-product. Users can use the data to create their own reports.

Because websites are used for decision-making purposes, and because of the growth of data-driven decision making, numerous company websites in their IR sections have contained various displays of data. This has taken the forms described in the following section.

Interactive Data Apps

Some companies use interactive data apps that contain data from the financial reports in some tabular form and can be downloaded into spreadsheets for analysis. For example, apps produced by Virtua Research of Boston, Massachusetts, are often used by companies to display financial statement data. Two examples, referred to on the websites as Interactive Analyst Centers, are Teck Resources[11] of Vancouver and Repligen Corporation[12] of Boston.

It is interesting to note that both example sites identify the analyst center as a separate linked site for which the company has "no control over the External Site, any data or other content contained therein or any additional linked websites." Although the companies provide the basic content, they do not administer or control the site and therefore cannot take responsibility for it.

Companies have been working hard to improve their IR websites to help investors deal with these challenges. They try to make their sites friendly, informative, and easy to navigate. Many have also been innovative in presenting information to investors in new and interesting ways. For example, the Data Tool in the site for Nutrien Inc.,[13] one of the leaders in financial reporting, represents a recognition that investors want to have data they can download and analyze on their own terms. Other leading companies like Agnico-Eagle[14] are doing the same.

Most companies have at the beginning of their IR section a series of key performance indicators, another way of presenting data. Often these indicators are unique to their industry and can help to provide a roadmap to the investor's investigation. Sections like the CEO's Report often speak to significant changes in these indicators. Of course, the financial statements are crucial and deserve a thorough reading. Many of the companies provide them in HTML format. The advantage of this, as opposed to the provision of PDF versions, is that individual items can be linked to relevant notes in the financial statements and the MD&A, which provide more explanation of the changes in the numbers and, in the case of the MD&A, more forward-looking information to help in making judgments about the future. And most of the websites include the proceedings of analyst conference calls, which often provide timely and relevant information about recent results and plans for the future.

Drilling down is a fundamental characteristic of the Web and drilling down from the key indicators to the detailed information that helps to explain them is a logical and effective means of investment analysis.

Key Performance Indicators

Key Performance Indicators that show single item data or comparisons, ratios, or percentages have been a significant part of the metrics used in evaluating business performance for many years. Examples of KPIs

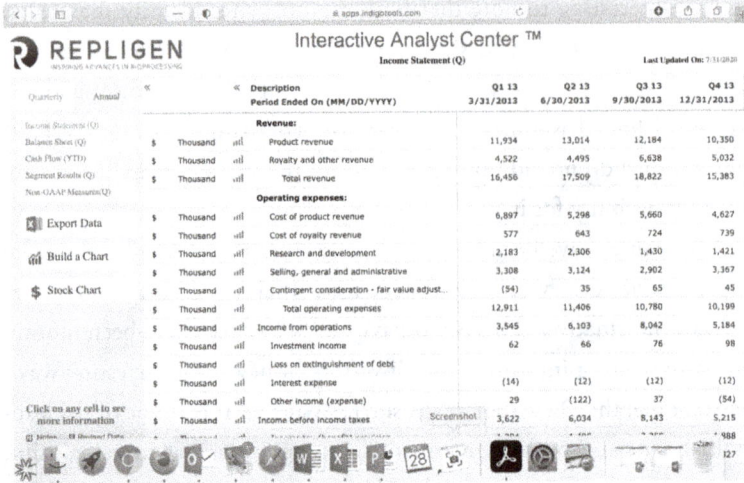

Figure 4.2 Repligen investor analyst center

are revenue per client (RPC), client retention rate (CRR), and profit margin (PM), income measures like EBIT (earnings before interest and tax) and EBITDA (earnings before interest, tax, depreciation, and amortization). Earnings per share can be considered a type of KPI as well and are generally the most widely quoted of all. Various items like this are shown on the Interactive Analyst Center of Repligen Corp.[15] (Figure 4.2)

KPIs are often shown on IR websites, often on the introductory page for financial information or in an otherwise prominent location.

Conclusion

The growing proliferation of data is only beginning to have a major impact on corporate reporting. We have seen how it has begun, with limited data disclosures on websites. But there is much more to come, particularly as companies learn to effectively use artificial intelligence to analyze the data and as investors learn to use AI and analytics in making their decisions.

CHAPTER 5

Static, Dynamic, and Interactive Data

Static versus Dynamic Data

Most information on websites is classified as static data, which may be defined as data that, once disclosed, does not change. Dynamic data, on the other hand, does change, often as new or updated data becomes available.

The problem with static data is that everything in the world changes. People change, as does their place of employment, age, income, preferences, and so on. Therefore, as soon as data are recorded, data decay sets in. The data become obsolete or, in the usual vernacular, lose quality. Many businesses have realized that they are trying to make decisions with low-quality data. Investment decisions are no different. Good, up-to-date data are necessary for making good investment decisions.

This is an important point for IR Sections in websites. If the objective is to provide data for making investment decisions, as it should be, then the data should be as dynamic as possible. For example, a presentation of monthly sales figures compared to previous months loses its relevance if there is no update after a month or two. One remedy is to add the latest month to the data to compare with previous months. It could also be done by having each column updated with each passing month, so that the display is always up-to-date. This would be a dynamic display solution.

Another example of dynamic data would be a graphic on sales and expenses that is linked to current records and updates periodically or even continuously as time moves on.

IR websites are ideally placed to present dynamic data for investors because the technology for websites can accommodate quick updates of information. The barrier has been the human factor; webmasters and website hosts are often busy and need time to do updates. But this can be automated and increasingly it is.

Interactive Data

Interactive data provide an opportunity for users to work with the data and sometimes even change them as they use them. This is often accomplished because of the inclusion of metadata in the data, which can be accessed by the user as desired. The SEC has used the term "interactive data" for several years to refer to XBRL (eXtensible Business Reporting Language), the electronic format required for filing corporate financial reports on EDGAR.

XBRL was inspired by Charles Hoffman, a practitioner from Tacoma, Washington. Around the turn of the century, he and a small group of accountants having the needed technical skills, developed the first iteration of the standard with the cooperation of the American Institute of Certified Public Accountants (AICPA). It was published in July 2000.

XBRL is a standards-based way to communicate and exchange business information between business systems. These communications are defined by metadata set out in taxonomies, which capture the definition of individual reporting concepts as well as the relationships between concepts and other semantic meanings.[1]

What this means in practical terms is that the concepts referred to are financial statement items, like cash, inventory, and sales revenue. The relationship between these concepts defined in the taxonomy is the relationships they have in compiling financial statements; for example, accounts receivable is one concept and allowance for doubtful accounts is another. The allowance is deducted from the accounts receivable (the relationship) to get net receivables (another concept).

Metadata in the form of identifying codes is added to the concepts; for example, the date and valuation. The concept of inventory might have, for example, metadata that shows the inventory is work in process, for X Company Ltd as at December 31, 2020 and is valued at lower of cost and net realizable value. This metadata always travels with the data, which adds to its usefulness. Without the metadata, the data would be just a meaningless number. In preparing financial information in XBRL format, the concepts and related information are all gathered together in one document, called the instance document.

In the jargon of interactive data, these identifying codes are called "tags."

> Of course, once identifying codes have been attached to each item of financial information in a company's SEC filing, computer software can search for and retrieve any of those items simply by searching for the corresponding tag—and do the same with hundreds or thousands of other filings more or less instantly.[2]

It's easy to see why the SEC wanted to use XBRL. They have so many filings to deal with, XBRL simply makes their job more doable. Also, the part of the tags (metadata) that defines relationships can be changed, with the necessary skills and tools, to yield different forms of reports than originally envisaged.

XBRL was never meant for human consumption, but just for processing by other computer systems. An XBRL instance document can be read by a human, but only after extensive education in the intricacies of XBRL. It is certainly not suitable for human investors unless it is fed into systems that they can then read in ordinary language. XBRL is very useful, however, because the computer systems that receive it can process it; for example, filings with the government, such as the SEC, can be readily checked without using valuable human resources and then the humans brought in to investigate apparent errors or other anomalies. This was one of the other important reasons the SEC required XBRL filings in the first place.

The fact that XBRL files cannot be read by humans has meant that filings with regulatory authorities had to be accomplished by two sets of files—conventional reports in a human readable language and XBRL files. Under this approach, the separate filings needed to be reconciled so they were both accurate and told the same story. This led to inefficiencies and errors. The solution for this dilemma was iXBRL.

Inline XBRL (iXBRL) is a form of XBRL that is readable to both machines and humans. With inline XBRL, only one report needed to be filed, because the XBRL tags could be included in the traditional HTML document, which meant the file could be read by people and also, since it would incorporate the XBRL tags, could be machine read.

One of the first and most successful implementations of inline XBRL was carried out in the UK by Companies House (the UK Registrar of companies) and HMRC (the UK tax department). In September, 2009, HMRC and Companies House issued a joint statement announcing a common approach to the online filing of company accounts that would utilize iXBRL. To help companies comply, they developed dedicated applications to help with the compilation of the filings. The new legislation meant that most companies would have to use iXBRL to file their Company Tax Returns, financial accounts and other computations for accounting periods after March 31, 2010.

In June 2018, the SEC passed a motion to amend their filing requirements to make a transition to inline XBRL. The plan was to phase-in the requirements such that large accelerated US GAAP filers would comply beginning with fiscal periods ending on or after June 15, 2019, accelerated filers for fiscal periods on or after June 15, 2020, and all other filers on or after June 15, 2021. The SEC also introduced an open source Inline XBRL Viewer to enable filers and the public to review and analyze the XBRL data more efficiently. Interestingly, the requirement for companies to post the XBRL data on their websites was eliminated at that time. The U.S. President had required that any new law had to be accompanied by the removal of two other requirements. Adding iXBRL meant removing the corporate website requirement as one of the two compromises.

The elimination of the requirement to disclose XBRL data on the corporate website may not be a bad idea, since a requirement for good IR websites is that a link to the EDGAR system be included so readers can go directly to that site for the SEC filings. This reduces duplication and also the possibility of error caused by producing two separate records of the same information.

The EU issued a directive in 2004 that set standards for companies listed to offer securities within the EU. In September 2018, guidelines setting the details of the new European Single Electronic Format (ESEF) were issued. This standard included a requirement to file with jurisdictional regulators using inline XBRL based on the new ESEF taxonomy (an adaptation of the IFRS taxonomy) for financial years beginning on or after January 1, 2020.

Inline XBRL was adopted in other countries as well:

- Japan's Financial Services Agency (JFSA) mandated XBRL in 2008 and this was later replaced with iXBRL in 2013.
- The Revenue Commissioners of Ireland initiated a voluntary program in 2012 for all tax payers to file their financial statements in inline XBRL. Mandatory filing was introduced in 2014.
- The Danish Business Authority, Denmark, introduced iXBRL in 2015.
- The Australian Securities and Investments Commission (ASIC) began an inline XBRL filing program in 2015.
- The Companies and Intellectual Property Commission (CIPC) in South Africa mandated inline XBRL with effect from July 2018.
- The SSM in Malaysia also passed a peremptory decree for qualifying companies to file in iXBRL.

Challenges of iXBRL

Since iXBRL is filed as one single file, it means the audit opinion expressed by auditors on the financial statements must be applied to the whole file, including the XBRL mark-ups or tags. Up until then, the audit issue could be avoided by having the auditors express their opinion on the traditional financial statements and not on the XBRL files. Some companies did get an opinion on the XBRL files, but this was rare.

The problem was that in expressing an opinion on the XBRL files, more audit work was required, such as:

- determining that the appropriate taxonomy was used;
- ensuring that the human-readable layer of the financial statements is identical to the audited information;
- determining whether the information embedded in the electronic report is marked-up in compliance with the regulatory requirements;
- evaluating any significant judgments made in reviewing tagging and use of taxonomies. For example, the matching of

financial statement items to the appropriate taxonomy items
often requires the exercise of judgment;

- ensuring that the audit procedures involved using the auditor's
understanding of a company's disclosure and business model
to ensure that the right tags were selected;
- ensuring that inappropriate extensions are not being used
and that relevant extensions are properly anchored to the
taxonomy.

The Committee of European Auditing Oversight Bodies (CEAOB)
published, in 2019, important guidance[3] for auditors reviewing financial
reports published in accordance with the new ESEF regulations.

To provide an opinion on whether or not financial statements comply with ESEF requirements, the auditor must both ensure that the
human-readable layer of the electronic report is audited *and* must determine whether the information embedded in the report is marked-up in
compliance with ESEF requirements. The guidelines state that, "taking
into account the materiality defined, the auditor should express an opinion (sometimes called 'positive' conclusion) on the compliance of the
marked-up information with the ESEF requirements."

In cases where the mark-ups are materially misstated, the auditor
should express a qualified or adverse opinion regarding this compliance.
The conclusion will depend on the severity and pervasiveness of the
misstatement(s).

A disclaimer of opinion on this compliance should be expressed, when
the auditor is unable to obtain sufficient appropriate evidence in this
regard. This step should improve both data quality and audit consistency
for ESEF filings.

Adoption of XBRL and iXBRL

When XBRL was first conceived and discussed by the financial and accounting professions, there was a degree of excitement that this new reporting
format had the potential to revolutionize financial reporting. There were
visions of investors receiving their financial statements in XBRL format
directly into their computers and then launching sophisticated analyses

themselves. There were visions of all financial reports using XBRL, and therefore being comparable and consistent, avoiding the traditional bane of financial reporting. All accountants would learn XBRL and teach it to their clients and employers.

It didn't quite work out that way. Companies found that implementing XBRL involved buying new tools and training staff in their use. It also meant adding new procedures to their financial reporting process, in order to do the tagging required. Given that XBRL files could not be read by people, the output of the process was regarded as limited in usefulness.

An exception to these concerns was the use of XBRL in regulatory filings. The regulators had long ago established standard type filings. And they had the resources to provide assistance to the filers in preparing the filings in XBRL. They also had the resources to develop and use advanced processing and analytical programs.

In the case of the UK and EU regulators, for example, the assistance to filers took the form of providing filing systems that automated much of the tagging and formatting required to complete the XBRL files. In the case of the SEC, the assistance was less extensive and involved providing some support to developers who created the tools necessary for filing. On the other hand, the SEC led the way in developing analytical programs that were used to analyze the filings and reveal any anomalies and errors.

In most cases, the filings were displayed on the regulators' websites, which substantially enhanced the volume and usefulness of financial information disclosed on the Internet. Some companies also have, as mentioned, disclosed the XBRL information on their own websites, and in some cases, such as SEC filers, were required to do so for several years.

However, when the SEC issued its June 2018 release on iXBRL, it noted that the XBRL information on corporate websites had not been used and users could get the information easily on EDGAR. It would, therefore, no longer be required on the corporate websites.

There was a substantial missed opportunity with the lack of use of XBRL on corporate websites. The data were in fact richer than basic numeric data and could be used in analytical tools more readily. However, no assistance was provided to website users in reading the data, which tools are available to do so, and could have been provided on the website. More importantly, some analytical tools could either be provided or referenced for use, which would have potentially been useful to the website users.

Perhaps with the introduction of iXBRL, this will change, since the disclosure will look the same to the users, and those who wish to make use of the XBRL component can do so. The iXBRL files can be read by users. For those who can use the XBRL component, they can use it for analysis. Either way, the website information using iXBRL would be useful. Moreover, even for those who are not disposed to using the XBRL for analysis, the data presented using iXBRL is much richer because it contains the metadata, which provides a good deal of additional information about the particular data points.

The corporate experience with the disclosure of XBRL information provides an additional example of the malaise that affects the use of corporate websites for corporate disclosure. This is the conception that websites are a vehicle for simply showing information and are only to be read by users—the paper paradigm. (Figure 5.1)

The paper paradigm holds companies back from fully participating in the information supply chain where data are available from internal and external records and then condensed and summarized into reports for the stakeholders. In the age of data-driven decision making, this chain of data should be an unbroken one where data are carried forward in a form such that the stakeholders can participate in the manner in which it is used, drawing out the data they need for decisions, moving it into their own

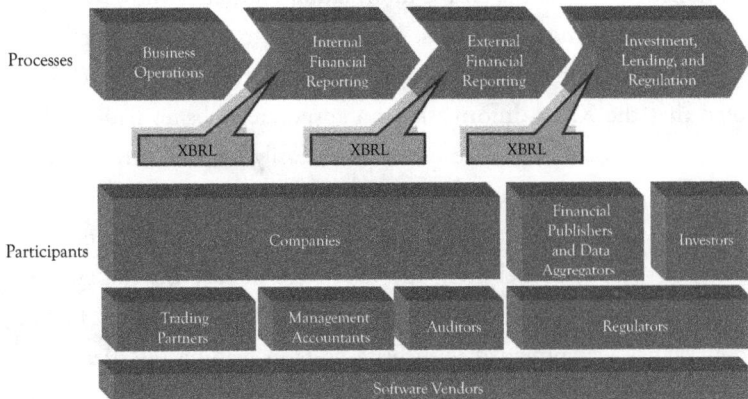

Figure 5.1 The Information Supply-chain

analytical tools and then creating their own reports most suitable for their purposes.

A full-blown recognition of data-driven decision making in the presentation of corporate websites would involve creating websites that are a rich source of data that are useful for analysis at the discretion of the users. It involves moving away from the idea of formulating complicated reports designed only to be read, toward the use of websites as a fully integrated part of the data supply chain. It need not be XBRL, but does need to be machine-readable data.

CHAPTER 6

Use of Graphics and Other Multimedia

Our discussion of data in corporate disclosure led us into a consideration of the use of graphics. One of the most prominent and useful characteristics of websites is the capacity to accommodate multimedia, which is defined as any combination of the five different types of media, including text, images, audio, video, and animation. Of course, text and images are the most widely used in traditional media, but websites accommodate all of them. Graphics are a form of multimedia as well, since they typically combine text and images. Graphics are widely used in websites and in traditional publications, but websites are particularly good at representing graphics and can include interactive graphics, such as those that provide a set of data and, with a single click, can convert the display from, for example, a bar chart to a line chart or a pie chart. Graphics are indispensable for representing financial data in user-friendly and useful forms.

Videos are commonly used on websites and for financial reporting are particularly useful for showing meetings such as analyst and shareholder meetings, and presentations such as those of executives and functional leaders, such as marketing, development, and plant maintenance.

Graphics

Graphics have been a substantial part of financial reporting for many years. They include traditional bar charts, line charts, pie charts, and so on. as well as geographical representations such as maps with numbers added to them for different geographical areas. Just about anything can be represented by the use of pictures combined with related numbers.

Because graphics use pictures rather than words, they can communicate results and ideas much more succinctly than plain text.

> Graphs are now used extensively, at least in the developed Western world. For example, Beattie and Jones [2001] demonstrate that 92% of Australian, 88% of French, 84% of German, 90% of Dutch, 82% of UK and 90% of US top companies use graphs in their annual reports.[1]

The study pointed out that companies use graphs for six reasons. They

1. allow management to present information in a flexible way;
2. are eye-catching;
3. are excellent at summarizing, distilling, and communicating financial information;
4. tap into a highly developed human cognitive skill, spatial intelligence;
5. are memorable (people remember pictures more easily than text and numbers); and
6. are egalitarian (they are largely independent of language, user sophistication, and nationality).

Videos and Slides

Videos have become an important part of communication of financial reporting. The most common medium for presenting them is YouTube, which enables videos to be prepared and embedded on websites.

YouTube and SlideShare are used for multimedia content, such as videos and presentations. Companies often use both of them for showing annual meetings and analyst meetings as well as the presentations made at those meetings and other presentations done by executives. These can be embedded on the website and become part of the corporate reporting effort.

YouTube's playlist feature enables content to be categorized. For example, a playlist could be devoted to annual meetings or shareholder meetings. Most other media also have categorization features, and this is a good way to enable a company to identify particular content as IR related.

An example of effective categorization can be found in Citibank, where 19 videos are classified under the playlist Financial and Economic Reports. Dell also makes good use of playlists as does TD Canada, although the latter has more general content than IR related material.

Benefits and Limitations of Using Graphics for Financial Reporting[2]

Graphics have the following benefits:

1. *Can be used to focus interest on key items* because their presence on a website draws the eye to them. Also, the choice of metrics can direct the attention of users to particular aspects on an issue. For example, a graphic on sales performance can be drawn that is based on absolute sales per week or on rate of growth per week. Each provides different information about the performance of sales and each will give a different impression.

2. *Attract and hold the attention of users*, especially if the graphic is interactive. For example, a graphic on sales per week can be presented for the company as a whole and provide buttons that can be clicked to switch the graphic to show sales per week for each of the regions of the company. For example, if one clicks the Eastern Region, the graphic will be changed to show the sales for that region. Similarly, a click of the Western or Central regions will change the graphic to show those regions. Also, the graphic can include buttons to show the percentage change in sales and portray the percentages instead of absolute dollars.

3. *Reduce information overload.* If a picture is worth a thousand words, then a picture can reduce the number of words used to disclose something, thereby reducing information overload.

4. *Reveal patterns and trends.* Patterns and trends are directly visible on a graphic, while on a written description, they may be more difficult to determine. Less analysis by the user is required to see trends and relationships on a graph.

5. *Help memory recall and message retention.* By reinforcing the textual stories and representing them in a different fashion, memory recall is likely to be improved. Research has reportedly shown that we remember visual images better than words. And "according to marketing industry influencer Krista Neher, the human brain can process images up to 60,000 times faster than words, and according to Forrester Research's Dr. James McQuivey, 'a minute of video is worth 1.8 million words.'"[3]

Limitations

Graphics have the following limitations:

1. *Be somewhat imprecise and therefore distort the accuracy of pure numbers.* Graphics and images depend more on impressions than on precision. For this reason, they are best read in conjunction with specific numbers.
2. *Be interpreted differently by different users.* Because of their imprecision, and reliance on impressions, users viewing them can take quite different messages from them.
3. *Present irrelevant information.* Images may include irrelevant information that draws attention away from the intended message.
4. *Focus on complex and picturesque designs, rather than key data.* People can get carried away with the fun and challenge of presenting the pictures and graphs in innovative ways and lose sight of the original intent of providing the best information.
5. *Inadvertently give false impressions.* For example, a picture of a factory might also include a pastoral country scene in the background which may give a false impression.
6. *If drawn improperly, unintentionally misrepresent the facts.* The classic case of this happening is where the x- and y-axis are scaled so as to alter the trends indicated by the data, whether by minimizing them or exaggerating them.
7. *Overuse of graphics can also take away from the impact.* We have been starting to see reports that are mostly graphics and one can reach a saturation point.

Table 6.1 Benefits and limitations of graphics in corporate reporting

Benefits	Limitations
Can be used to focus interest	Can be imprecise and distort accuracy
Attract attention of users	Can be open to various interpretations
Reduce information overload	Can include irrelevant information
Reveal patterns and trends	Can focus on design rather than key data
Help memory recall	Can give false impressions
	Improper design can distort the facts

Overall, despite their limitations, graphics and images present an opportunity for financial presentations to be more attractive and more interesting to readers. To address these issues, companies should define the message carefully, and use care in selecting the type of graphic and designing it. They also need to review the graphics and images for the accuracy of the messages they convey.

There have been numerous research papers on the use of graphics to communicate information. One of particular interest to IR websites explored the effect of different characteristics of digital content, such as design, scenario, structure, musicality, and entertainment value of digital content, on the value assigned to it by users. Their findings suggest that these characteristics have a significant effect on the value of digital content. "Users of digital content become absorbed emotionally in the contents by means of elements such as musicality and entertainment value. Sound effects and background music appropriate for a situation can affect users' responses and allow them to experience flow. When the contents bring about more fun, entertainment, and interest, the sense of flow can be increased. Digital content can be seen as a synthetic entity composed of text, sound, video, scenario and structure."[4]

In a 2012 study carried out by Cho, Michelon, and Patten, considerable evidence was found of "both enhancement and obfuscation in the use of graphs. More than 70 percent of the graphs included in the standalone reports depict items with a favorable underlying trend. Similarly, for those graphs constructed with material distortion (based on the relative graph discrepancy (RGD) index) more than 60 percent are biased in a direction that is favorable to the company (overemphasizing positive trends or underemphasizing negative ones)."[5] The study focused on sustainability reports, but it sets out a scenario that could well apply to any corporate reporting. Numerous studies have shown that graphs are often used to obfuscate information or enhance favorable trends. Many of them are documented in the study by Beattie et al.[6]

A very simple example of the use of graphics can be found in the website of Daimler on https://daimler.com/investors/key-figures/divisions/ (Figure 6.1).

€ 40,281 mn	€ 3,070 mn	€ 2,158 mn
Revebye	EBIT	Net profit
Q3 2019: € 43,270 mn	Q3 2019: € 2,690 mn	Q3 2019: € 1,813 mn

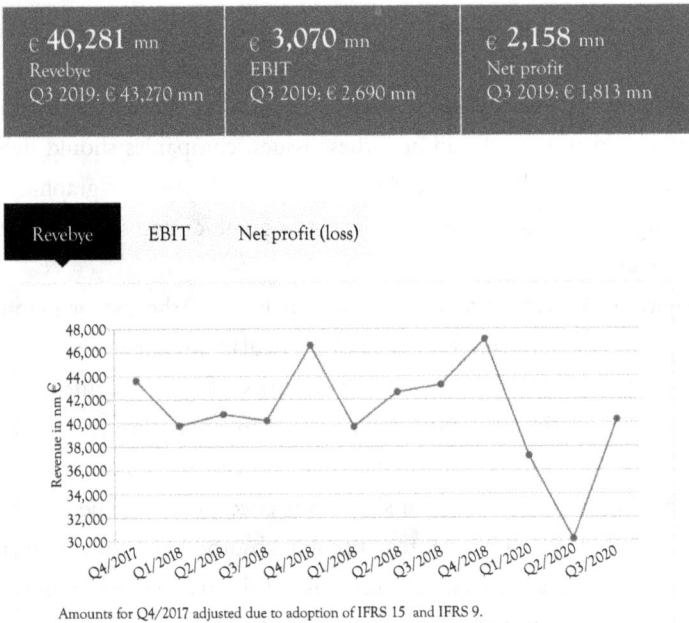

Figure 6.1 Daimler quarterly results

It is an interactive graph in the sense that if a cursor is placed on a point in the graph, a box appears showing the exact number of units sold in the particular quarter. Many examples of similar interactive graphs can be found in corporate websites.

All those studies which report the frequency distribution of Graph Discrepancy Indices (except for Steinbart [1989]) showed more overstatements of trends than understatements. Beattie and Jones's [1992a] findings are typical, showing 22 material exaggerations and 8 material understatements.[7]

Relationship of Graphics to Analysis

Financial reports are meant to be analyzed, not just read. When data are analyzed, graphics is the most widely used tool for visualization. With modern reporting it often is the case that users prepare their own graphics from the data provided to them. Quite often they need to extract the data from a variety of forms, such as text, and then convert the data into something useful. The use of applications like Tableau is accelerating this trend. The use of interactive data or XBRL can be helpful in this process, since the data can then be read by computers, saving the humans a lot of work. With good Internet-based reporting, there is an opportunity to interface with analysts to help them in their work.

They can do this in several ways. They can provide disaggregated data in a form that can be downloaded and used. This does not work in PDF forms, but does when numbers are included in the HTML sections of the website. Companies generally provide such data through the use of separate data banks or data tools as described in Chapter 5.

They can also provide analytical tools that can assist analysts and other users with their analytical work. An excellent example of a website where such tools are provided is that of BP at https://bp.com/en/global/corporate/investors.html. This can be seen on the page https://bp.com/en/global/corporate/investors/investor-tools.html

Companies have made a start in this respect by providing financial statements and other data in an Excel format. Several companies have been taking this approach. Of course, the idea is that the data can be downloaded into the user's own spreadsheets and analyzed. The usefulness of the data is much improved in this way.

Companies should be presenting data so it can be used and not just read. This means that the data needs to be presented as data and not in text or forms like PDF files where the data cannot be extracted at all. Tools for analysis are available that are much more sophisticated than spreadsheets, such as Tableau and the others mentioned earlier. If corporate websites include data that can be easily downloaded into these tools, the usefulness of the corporate disclosures would be much enhanced.

Conclusions

Graphics have been an important part of corporate reporting for many years. However, the advent of big data and advanced analytics is leading to an increase in their use and complexity. Overall this is a positive development for corporate reporting, but there are pitfalls to avoid.

CHAPTER 7

Use of Social Media and Blogs

Corporate financial reporting in recent years has extended far beyond corporate websites to include social media. Some use Facebook and have their own Facebook page. Use of Twitter is common, especially for such short items as earnings and dividend announcements and other news events. YouTube is also common for use in showing videos of company gatherings, including investor meetings and executive presentations. LinkedIn, since it is populated heavily by professionals, is used for a variety of financial reports. Several companies use blogs, although blogs devoted to IR are much less common; most of them are marketing devices.

Social media are also used by companies for promotional purposes well beyond the realm of corporate financial reporting and sometimes it is difficult to distinguish these uses—whether a particular disclosure item is a part of the formal financial reports or simply marketing. Websites are also used for both promotional and reporting purposes, but the use of Investor Relations sections helps considerably in determining whether the purpose of the disclosures is financial reporting or promotional. Also, the companies often insert warning pop-ups for users when they stray beyond the company website while seeking information or following links.

Social media have transformed how people interact and socialize online. Therefore, every company needs to consider how the social media tools can be leveraged in a business environment.

Social media tools represent opportunities for any company. Users can access the Internet at home, in the office, or on their phone. It is now easier than ever for a company to directly target customers with marketing campaigns, offer new online services, or build brand awareness through the use of blogs and social networking sites. Similarly, use of social media enables a company to create a community and converse online with investors and other stakeholders.

Dialogue between a Company and Stakeholders

Because of this Web culture, stakeholders have come to expect timely content and considerable variety, including audio and video, podcasts, blogs, online forums. and social networking. This can sometimes involve a two-way dialogue between the stakeholders and the business.

An early proponent of the corporate dialogue concept was Barry Spaul, in a study done for the Institute of Chartered Accountants in England and Wales.[1]

As he explained it, the concept encompasses the ideas of:

- bi-directional flows of information between a variety of participants and
- information flows managed by AI that can determine the information needs of particular groups.

Since then we have seen information flows become bidirectional through the use of social media, which normally allows for the inclusion of comments by readers and replies or comments by management or other employees. Now, in 2020, we are seeing the emergence of AI for a variety of purposes, and while the use of AI for financial reporting has not been widely apparent on the Internet, it is likely that it will soon become common, given the strong interest in AI throughout society and within many companies.

The Web has raised stakeholder expectations. They expect immediacy in their online interactions, look for regularly updated content, and anticipate timely responses to any comments.

An in-depth survey was undertaken in 2009 to consider the use of social media in general.[2] Key findings from consumers/users were as follows:

- 49 percent use social media at least once a day;
- 31 percent of consumers agree that social media are more credible than advertising;
- 61 percent are researching products to purchase;
- 36 percent depend on social media to help them with purchase decisions;

- 40 percent are "talking" to or learning from specific organizations;
- 25 percent of users feel better about an organization engaged in social media.

Although the survey is a bit dated now, nevertheless, it shows relationships that existed at that time and likely extend to the present.

In September 2009, *IR Alert* conducted a survey of 270 IR professionals to establish a benchmark of social media usage by Investor Relations Officers (IROs) and Chief Financial Officers (CFOs).[3] The results of the survey indicate that about 60 percent of industry professionals use social media in some way, especially those who work at smaller firms. Only 12 percent of IRO and CFO respondents indicated that they use social media to disseminate financial information to shareholders and the market. Of the various social networks, Twitter is the most used by investor relations professionals to communicate their messages.

Other highlights of this survey are as follows:

- Although conference calls and news releases remain a commonly used method of communicating investor relations information to shareholders and the market, about 6.3 percent of respondents now use a corporate blog to communicate financial information, while 13.6 percent of companies with annual sales of less than $50 million use one.
- Most public companies do not use any form of social media for communicating financial information. In fact, only 12.5 percent of respondents said they use social media to communicate with shareholders and the market.
- Twitter is the most-used social network for this purpose, used by about 79 percent of social-media-engaged respondents.
- LinkedIn is by far the most popular social network among investor relations professionals, with almost 80 percent of social-media-engaged respondents using it at least once a month.

In August 2009, Q4 Web Systems issued a research report analyzing 80 public companies and their use of Twitter during the second quarter

2009 earnings season. The research shows that the number of public companies with Twitter accounts grew by 270, or 338 percent. Of these, the number using Twitter for investor relations (IR) increased by 77 or 175 percent. Although still small in terms of the potential universe, the research indicates that social networks are an effective medium with which to reach out and interact with stakeholders.[4]

What is usually posted on Twitter as far as IR is concerned?[5] According to the research report:

- 53 percent provided a link to their earnings release only;
- 18 percent provided a link to their notice of call and earnings release only;
- 8 percent provided a link to their notice of call, earnings release, and webcast;
- 7 percent provided a link to their earnings release and webcast only.

Use of social media by companies for investor relations purposes is more limited. For example, in 2013, Q4 Inc did a survey of 890 companies[6] to see what social media they used. They found that of the 890 companies in their sample:

- 72 percent use Twitter for investor-related material (up 9 percent from their 2012 study).
- 45 percent use Facebook for investor-related material (up 5 percent).
- 52 percent use SlideShare for investor-related material (up 8 percent).
- 42 percent use YouTube for investor-related material (up 13 percent).
- 32 percent use their corporate blog for investor-related material (up 14 percent).
- 66 percent of companies are listed on StockTwits
- 82 percent of companies have their social media links on their corporate website (up 17 percent).

In the FTSE 100, 72 companies shared their financial results on Twitter during 2017, up from 69 in 2016. Exactly half (50) shared their results through LinkedIn, up from 42 the year before, and 23 companies created results-oriented videos for YouTube, up from 18.[7]

In 2018, for 2017, "FTI Consulting's Index—its fifth annual edition—shows a startling 105 percent increase over the previous year in interactions with results-related content from FTSE 100 companies posted through Twitter, LinkedIn, YouTube and SlideShare."[8]

The statistics show that LinkedIn has seen a dramatic increase in usage for investor relations purposes in recent years. Other statistics also show that 85 percent of investors check into LinkedIn at least monthly. Probably it's a lot more frequently than that.[9]

These statistics are quite impressive, both for the extent of usage of social media for IR (therefore for corporate reporting) and for the obvious trends from the prior year, showing significant increases in all categories.

The use of social media (SM) by companies for corporate reporting has been growing in recent years. Facebook, Twitter, YouTube, Flickr, SlideShare, StockTwits, Blogs, Google+, Pinterest, and LinkedIn have all been used in varying degrees and in different ways.

The use of social media for reporting purposes was of incidental interest until April 2013, when the U.S. Securities and Exchange Commission issued a press release stating that:

> … companies can use social media outlets like Facebook and Twitter to announce key information in compliance with Regulation Fair Disclosure (Regulation FD) so long as investors have been alerted about which social media will be used to disseminate such information.[10]

Regulation FD is the key SEC rule that seeks to ensure that no group of investors is favored in the provision of information. The objective is to ensure a level playing field for all investors. The reference to Reg FD in the SEC announcement is important, as it allows the company to use social media for primary announcements, provided the shareholders have been informed as to which social media will be used so they will know where to look for the information.

Since the SEC opened the way to formal notices being sent out by social media, many companies have been exploring ways to use these vehicles.

Role of Social Media

"Social media" generally refers to a number of specific websites, including Facebook, Twitter, YouTube, SlideShare, StockTwits, and LinkedIn. There are several others in popular use, especially by young people, but these particular sites have entered the mainstream in business. Blogs are also considered to be social media, although some people consider them as becoming obsolete.

During recent U.S. presidential elections, the overall importance of social media in the distribution of information and knowledge became more apparent. Twitter, which seems to be a most favored vehicle for purpose of elections, has been used in several elections in the past, notably those of 2012, 2014, and 2016.

The U.S. elections made clear two major points about social media. It is a powerful tool, enabling a person or group to make his or her message known to others without resorting to the conventional media. If the user is widely known, such as a candidate in an election, then something like Twitter can be a very powerful tool.

It has also been made clear that people have a hard time determining the truth of postings in social media. There is nothing new about this and research has shown over recent years that people generally place greater faith in the conventional media than in social media. They often will obtain a lot of information from social media but when something particularly important is happening, they will turn to conventional news because it is written by professional journalists. That being said, there is a subset of the population that doesn't trust the conventional media either.

Against this background, public companies know they will be discussed in social media and have to be aware that fictitious news will be circulated about them, which sometimes could be harmful. Accordingly, they need to decide whether and how they are going to tell their own story.

Types of Information Disclosed Through Social Media

It is important to note that use of social media for purposes of investor relations is a concept that can be somewhat ambiguous. For example, there is information that is clearly investor related, such as earnings reports, or notices of shareholder meetings. This might be called Type 1 IR information. Then there is other information that is simply of interest to investors, even though it may not have been directed to investors. This might include information on new products, new business arrangements, or geographical information. This might be called Type 2 IR information.

So how do companies actually use social media? We address this issue by type of social media, starting with Twitter and StockTwits.

Twitter is, as seen above, the most heavily used of all the social media for corporate reporting. Although Twitter is limited to 280 characters, it can be used to convey weblinks, which gives it the capacity to convey large amounts of information.

Twitter is being used by several companies for

- Earnings and corporate actions announcements
- Questions for conference calls
- Event promotion
- Live-tweeting of annual and quarterly meetings

Examples include Alcoa, Pepsi, Starbucks, Coca-Cola Company, Boeing, eBay, and BASF.

StockTwits

Many public companies are incorporating the use of StockTwits to help increase awareness and broaden access to their company information.

- Of the sample of 890 companies in the Q4 survey, 66 percent have a presence on StockTwits.
- Examples are Ford Company and Royal Bank of Canada.

Starbucks won an award from the national Investor Relations Institute in 2013 for its use of social media in IR. One of the strong reasons for this success was its "Starbucks News" account on Twitter, which contains a good deal of IR information. This is still available at @StarbucksNews.

Another similar example was the "Dellshares" account of Dell Corp (https://twitter.com/DellShares), which also contained considerable amounts of IR information before the shares were taken off NASDAQ in 2013. Dell can now be found under the hashtag @Dell. Cisco Inc. makes good use of Twitter as well under @Cisco.

Facebook and LinkedIn

Facebook is used less than Twitter, but more than others. Most of the use of Facebook is directed to general marketing and does not usually contain much in the way of technical information. However, some companies, presumably because of the overall popularity of Facebook, do include some investor-related information.

Goldcorp makes extensive use of social media, including use for IR purposes. The Goldcorp Facebook site links to a blog which link in turn contains a feed of the Twitter tweets issued by/on Goldcorp. Also, that same page contains links to the other social media used by Goldcorp, which include the full blog "Above Ground," YouTube, SlideShare, and Flickr.

This is a good example of how some companies are using social media on an integrated basis, exploiting the particular characteristics of each form of media and linking them so users can get a full view of the events or matters they wish to disclose.

The reliability of social media is often questioned, and for good reason. Many entries are made about a company by people with no connection to that company and who have no particular knowledge nor expertise. Naturally the information they put on social media has a high possibility of being unreliable. However, often a company enters information itself, and this information is likely to be as reliable as any of the formal information it places on its annual report or other official media. Therefore, in considering social media for investor information, it makes sense to give particular attention to information issued by the company. In order to preserve the integrity of the information about it, some companies will set aside special corporate accounts for their social media content and exclude or prohibit any information from outside sources.

LinkedIn is a favorite social media for business professionals and one that can be used effectively for investor relations. Strangely, it has not yet achieved the level of use for IR that Twitter and Facebook have. However, some companies maintain corporate sites on LinkedIn and they do often have notices such as earnings releases and conference calls. An example is Agrium Inc.

Examples of Companies Using Social Media

Many international companies have become active participants in social media. A recent Burson-Marsteller Fortune Global 100 Social Media Study found that 79 percent of the largest 100 companies in the Fortune Global 500 index are using at least one of the most popular social media platforms: Twitter, Facebook, YouTube, or corporate blogs. Approximately 65 percent of these companies have active accounts on Twitter, 54 percent have a Facebook Fan Page, 50 percent have a YouTube channel, and 33 percent have corporate blogs (though not necessarily IR blogs). About 20 percent are utilizing all four platforms to engage with stakeholders. In Canada, companies such as Barrick Gold Corporation, Canada Gas Corp., and TVI Pacific Inc. see value in using social media and they have incorporated it into their online communications plans.

Barrick Gold Corporation began using Twitter in October 2008 to increase the level of interaction between the company and its stakeholders. It uses Twitter to circulate news release headlines, providing a link to the full release. Over time, it began receiving questions and comments in @ replies and direct messages, and responded to them as they arrived. After gaining comfort with the medium, Barrick Gold increased its posts and interacted with followers more. It also followed related social media to stay up-to-date.

Barrick Gold provides Tweets about upcoming events, new content posted on the website, reminders of quarterly earnings announcements, and conference calls. In April 2009, it launched a Twitter feed specifically for recruiting purposes (@barrickgoldjobs), in which it posts employment opportunities, links followers to the Careers section of its website, and responds to questions from potential candidates. It also launched an official Facebook page for recruiting activities.

Canada Gas Corp. is listed on the TSX-venture exchange, the Frankfurt exchange, and the OTC Bulletin Board. Currently, it uses Twitter, Facebook, and LinkedIn, and encourages forum participation. As the company continues to evolve, it foresees using video blogging or some kind of shareholder forum. Among venture-listed companies using social media, Canada Gas is one of the early adopters and has been helping others understand their potential in this area.

In a recent development, Canadian-based copper producer TVI Pacific Inc. has recognized the discussion board on the company's Facebook page as its "official Corporate Discussion Forum." Since launching its Facebook page in November 2009, the company's Facebook discussion board has developed into a key communication channel between TVI and its investors.

By officially adopting the Facebook discussion board, TVI is now drawing all investors' attention to the fact that the forum is a formal part of the company's communications program. It was important to do this so that all investors are made aware of the discussion board's existence and have an opportunity to review the information the company is providing on it. Access to view the discussion board is open to the public and all information on it is exposed to public search engines such as Google. TVI does not use the forum to disclose material nonpublic information.

According to TVI's executive director of investor relations,

TVI decided to adopt Facebook as its "official" corporate discussion forum for two reasons. First, it is an effective way to correct the facts. When we notice, on public chat rooms like Stockhouse Bullboards, incorrect information about TVI, we post a discussion topic and simply post the correct information. I know it works because I will see a post on the Billboards a short time later quoting the correct information. This has been very effective in keeping the facts straight.

The second reason is that it's important for us to develop relationships with our shareholders and by using Facebook, we can identify with them without the "anonymous factor." Shareholders who are personally or emotionally attached to a company tend to be more loyal and less likely to spook in a downturn.

Usefulness of Social Media for Reporting

While it is well known that social media is widely used generally, the question arises as to whether investors use it. Much research has been done on social media usage, and statistics on such usage have been made available from a variety of sources.

Work done by Pew Research, for example, shows that 74 percent of online adults use social media.[11]

The fastest growing demographic on both Facebook and Google+ was the 45–54 age group, at a rate of 46 percent and 56 percent respectively.[12] Similarly, on Twitter the 55–64 year age bracket is the fastest growing demographic cohort with a 79 percent growth rate.

For particular groups of interest, however, the statistics show a different story. For example, a study done by the National Investor Relations Institute (NIRI) revealed that analysts don't use social media much. They feel it is not reliable but did say that the most reliable form of SM is Corporate Blogs. In addition, the majority of survey respondent IR professionals (72 percent) said they do not use social media for their IR work.

Another survey, however, conducted by Q4 Inc, who are specialists in electronic corporate reporting, found that, consistent with the results of NIRI's 2010 social media study, respondents report not using social media for IR primarily due to lack of interest by the investment community. This survey also found, however, that the interest of IR professionals is growing. Almost half (49 percent) who do not currently use social media in their IR program plan to reassess the issue within the next 12 months.

Among investors, a Q4 survey showed that 52 percent of survey contributors utilize social media as part of their research process, a slightly smaller number than 2010 levels of 56 percent. The vast majority of these respondents indicate that it has influenced their investment decisions at least occasionally.

According to an article on the PricewaterhouseCoopers website, "Social media: time for reporters to join the conversation," by Mehdi and Palmer, "Around 50% of professional investors in the US regularly use blogs and follow each other on Twitter and StockTwits, and more than 60% of institutional investors say that social media will become increasingly important to them."

Most analysts, 92 percent, consider the information gleaned from social media sites as either somewhat or not at all reliable. According to the entire survey group, it is the lowest rated information source in terms of influence.

In light of the SEC's decision to grant credibility to postings on sites such as Facebook and Twitter, 43 percent of analysts assert they will likely utilize social media more often as part of their research process. Financial blogs, including Seeking Alpha, as well as LinkedIn and Twitter, are viewed as the most valuable social media resources; only 25 percent find company-sponsored blogs useful.

Challenges and Best Practices

In all social media, best practice calls for a dedicated presence as opposed to an ad hoc one on various other accounts. There is a clear need to distinguish between official corporate entries and those of other people. This is best accomplished by having a corporate account complete with logos and other material and images that clearly identify it as an official corporate account. In addition, the account needs to be monitored closely by responsible employees to weed out the spam and inappropriate comments (if comments are allowed). All social media have a search facility so the entries should be labelled clearly and properly to enable the search engines to direct users as accurately as possible.

Best Practices Entries on Twitter

Twitter is known for utilizing hashtags such as #pepsico, #starbucks or #investors for its entries. Hashtags are very useful for helping users find entries and for categorizing tweets. As with all social media, entries should be official corporate notifications and made only by authorized people. Although Twitter is restricted to 240 characters, it does permit the inclusion of weblinks, which makes it possible to effectively use it to send out much larger pieces of information than the 240 characters and also makes it possible to stream events using weblinks to YouTube or other streaming media.

Best Practices on Facebook

Facebook is not widely used as a vehicle for corporate reporting, although a great many organizations use it for marketing purposes. If it is used, the same rules apply as for other social media: have a dedicated administrator, make the entries as official corporate entries and differentiate the corporate entries from those of others.

Best Practices on YouTube

YouTube enables the use of playlists which facilitate the grouping of videos under appropriate and relevant headings. For example, executive announcements can be grouped together, as can all videos for a particular fiscal year.

YouTube provides for separate corporate channels that can be used as a local rallying point and a convenient location for related videos. Finding relevant information on social media is always an issue, although all the media have search engines. But search engines aren't always enough.

Some of the companies help their users by providing indexes and customized search facilities. Siemens is a good example of this in their use of YouTube. That company provides playlists that classify the video content by topic. Although they are not restricted to investor relations, many of the playlists can be identified as likely relevant to investing. For example, the playlist for industrial productivity should be of interest to investors.

Conclusions

Companies have been using social media for corporate reporting purposes with increasing frequency. Each of the popular media has a useful purpose and the use of social media needs to be carefully planned and managed in order to be effective. There should be objectives and plans of action and proper oversight.

CHAPTER 8

Impact of Device Types

Various types of devices can be used to access information on the Internet. This is a fact that needs to be recognized in Internet reporting. These include mobile units, desktop computers, and tablets. These are the most common types, but there are more, and some of the others are or may be growing in importance. Consider, for example, smart wrist watches, smart TVs, pod players, Google Home units, eBook readers, and game consoles.

Desktop computers are still a very common way to access the Internet. However, they are no longer the most common. That place was taken by mobile phones in recent years. A Q4 study for 2011 showed that:

- Mobile traffic grew 2.3-fold in 2011, making it the fourth year in a row that mobile traffic has more than doubled.
- Perhaps even more staggering, mobile traffic in 2011 was eight times the size of the entire global Internet traffic in 2000.
- Also in 2011, smartphone use tripled, with the average amount of traffic per smart phone being 150 MB per month, while it had been only a 55 MB average in 2010.

Americans continue to be more likely to get news through mobile devices than through desktop or laptop computers. Roughly six-in-ten U.S. adults (57%) often get news this way, compared with 30 percent who often do so on a desktop or laptop computer, according to a Pew Research Center survey.[1]

The share of Americans aged 18 to 29 who often get news from a mobile device has more than doubled since 2013, increasing from 34 percent then to 72 percent today. During the same period, the share of Americans aged 18 to 29 who often get news from a desktop or laptop computer has decreased 9 percentage points (from 34% in 2013 to 23% in 2019). The two middle age groups, those aged 30 to 49 and 50 to 64, have followed a similar pattern.[2]

The way that people consume content on a daily basis has drastically changed over the past ten years. The article notes that there has been an obvious shift from the use of conventional, immobile PCs, to devices like smartphones and tablets that cater to the needs of professionals on-the-go. Investor Relations Officers (IROs) should actively encourage the concept of connectivity and adopt it when communicating to their investor and analyst audience, if they aren't already doing so.[3]

Investment Relations Officers cannot ignore the statistics that show the financial services industry (particularly financial advisors) are the leading users of tablets in a business setting:

- 40 percent of financial professionals have an iPad.
- 59.3 percent use the iPad in client meetings.
- 48.9 percent say the iPad helps them be more responsive to clients.[4]

Usage of computers, including tablets, for the Internet is different from that of mobile phones. Browsing the Web on phones used to be very limited and awkward. Many mobile phones could only use micro-browsers, such as WAP (Wireless Application Protocol). But the browsing capabilities of phones have progressed in recent years. Now there are several mobile browsers that offer users an experience comparable to desktop browsing, albeit with a smaller screen.

The small screen raises a number of issues. For example, large displays of data cannot be seen very easily on smartphone screens. This limits the usefulness of the data because they cannot be analyzed on a smartphone since the visibility and capability of analysis are both lacking. The main usefulness of the phones is in their ability to browse and read reports. For some investors, this is enough. For others, in particular those who engage in real analysis, it is not.

Tablets offer an experience with browsing very similar to that of computers and accordingly have become much more common. Usually they have a smaller screen, but being bigger than most phones, they are not as much of a problem. They are good for reading more complex reports and can also be used to do simple analysis.

Smart TVs typically come equipped with Internet connectivity and the ability to read websites and access online video services like YouTube, Hulu, and Netflix. They often include Web browsers that offer some kind of Web browsing experience, which varies depending on make.

Game consoles like Xbox and Nintendo all come equipped with Web browsers that allow the user to access websites. While not the most convenient nor the most likely to be used for analyzing annual reports, nevertheless, it is possible. Smart TVs and game consoles can also be used to access online video services, and videos are often used for corporate reporting purposes.

Wristwatches include Android Wear and Apple Watches. Apps to run Web browsers can be installed on an Android watch. Apple Watch doesn't have a browser yet, but likely will have in the future. Of course, the browser experience on these units will be even more limited than that on smart phones.

Ebook readers like the Amazon Kindle can connect to the Internet, primarily to enable the owner to browse and purchase books. There is also a browser available with limited capability.

Cars have a screen on their dashboard that can be used to accommodate a Web browser but it's not common because of the potential to distract drivers. Nevertheless, some, like the Tesla Web Browser and the Pioneer CarBrowser App, can be used to browse the Web.

The Shift to Mobile Units

Because the use of portable devices such as smartphones and tablets has increased dramatically over recent years, they are the most likely to be used by investors for at least scanning corporate websites and so they need to be taken into account in designing websites.

In a series of surveys done in 2019, Pew Research showed that "the vast majority of Americans—96 percent—now own a cellphone of some kind. The share of Americans that own smartphones is now 81 percent, up from just 35 percent in Pew Research Center's first survey of smartphone ownership conducted in 2011."[5]

Of course, there are variations in the population regarding the extent of ownership, the principal variants being age, education, and income. As one might expect, younger people tend to have more smartphones than older ones. Ninety-six percent of people aged 18–29 years owned a smartphone, as opposed to 92 percent of people aged 30–49, 79 percent of those aged 50–64, and 53 percent of those over 65. People with higher education also tend to have smartphones more often, as do people with higher incomes.

A growing share of Americans now use smartphones as their primary means of online access at home. Today roughly one-in-five American adults are "smartphone-only" Internet users, meaning they own a smartphone, but do not have traditional home broadband service. This makes it even more important to make sure that the company website works well on smartphones.

Some of those users use their smartphone for investing purposes. Noteworthy is the adoption of investing apps like Betterment by people primarily between the ages of 18 and 34. One survey found that 31 percent say they have at least one investing app on their phone. Some investors also use the bank investor sites. This differs from the online banking access, which a majority of people use regularly. This grew particularly during the pandemic when people were trying to avoid personal contact. However, many of the banks, and most of the large ones, have their own online investing products and of course there are apps to use in researching and executing potential purchase transactions. Given the increase in smartphone usage, It Is reasonable to expect that these investment apps are also being used more often on phones. It's not a large leap for such users to begin using their phones to go into corporate websites as part of their research.

An expected $30 trillion is expected to be transferred to millennials as they inherit their parents' and grandparents' money. When that happens, where they will invest will be a major point of interest for traditional wealth managers. Will they stick with the robo-advisory firm that charged them low fees when all they could afford to invest was, say, $50 a month? Or will they go where their parents banked? This question is prompting numerous banks and wealth managers to produce a variety of online solutions.

This is instructive from the viewpoint of web-based financial information. Investments in stocks and bonds generally increase with age and therefore vary inversely with smartphone ownership. People with higher incomes also tend to invest more. Although it cannot be assumed that the use of smartphones for reading IR websites varies directly with smartphone usage, it is reasonable to assume intuitively that such usage does at least increase with smartphone ownership. Based on statistics like this, most observers have concluded that smartphones are a growing factor in the consumption of financial information disclosed on websites.

What this means for IR websites is that the IR sites need to be easily read on smartphones and tablets. This is normally achieved by making them responsive.

Responsive Websites

Responsive Web design is the approach that suggests that design and development should respond to the user's behavior and environment based on screen size, platform, and orientation.

A responsive website means that a website is easily readable and navigable to people who use a laptop, an iPad, or iPhone, Android device, or any other. The website should automatically change format to accommodate the resolution, image size, and scripting abilities of the particular device being used. This eliminates the need for a different design and development phase for each new gadget on the market.

One good example of a responsive website is that of Barrick Gold.

Barrick's site automatically moves its top tool bar navigation into a dropdown menu option as the screen gets smaller. This way, the user is still able to have access to all the navigational abilities they have on the desktop oriented view, without crowding the screen.[6]

Responsive sites address not only the navigational aspects of the site but also provide for changes in the way the sites handle content.

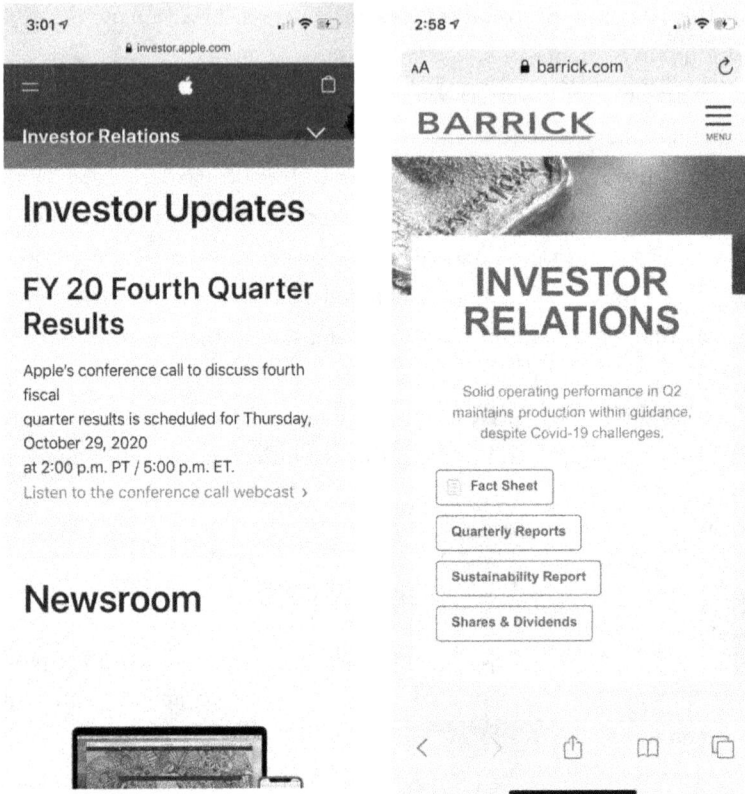

Figure 8.1 Investor websites on a smartphone

In Barrick's case, as the screen gets smaller, the website automatically stacks information like lists and charts so that it is easily scrolled through on a mobile device. Side filters like sorting information by date can also be stacked so the user can easily select what time frame of information they are looking for.[7]

Responsive websites are essential for companies that wish to have their websites taken seriously by users with smartphones or tablets. If users attempt to use websites that are not responsive, the site often will not fit the screen, will be difficult or impossible to navigate and generally be unintelligible to many users. Accordingly, most IR websites are responsive.

It is important to note that while responsiveness of websites is essential to maximize the usefulness of smartphones for Web browsing, it does not solve the problem of limitations in analytical ability. Investors interested in doing serious analysis will need to use a desktop or laptop computer with the necessary tools installed.

Investor Relations Apps

Another reporting technique that has been employed by a number of companies is the production of Investor Relations apps that are designed for smartphones and tablets. They can be obtained at the Apple Apps Store (for iPads and iPhones) and the Google Play Site (for Android tablets and phones). While mobile applications for smartphones and tablets for investor relations are a relatively new concept, the market for them has grown very quickly over the last year (2011) on a global scale.[8] (Figure 8.2).

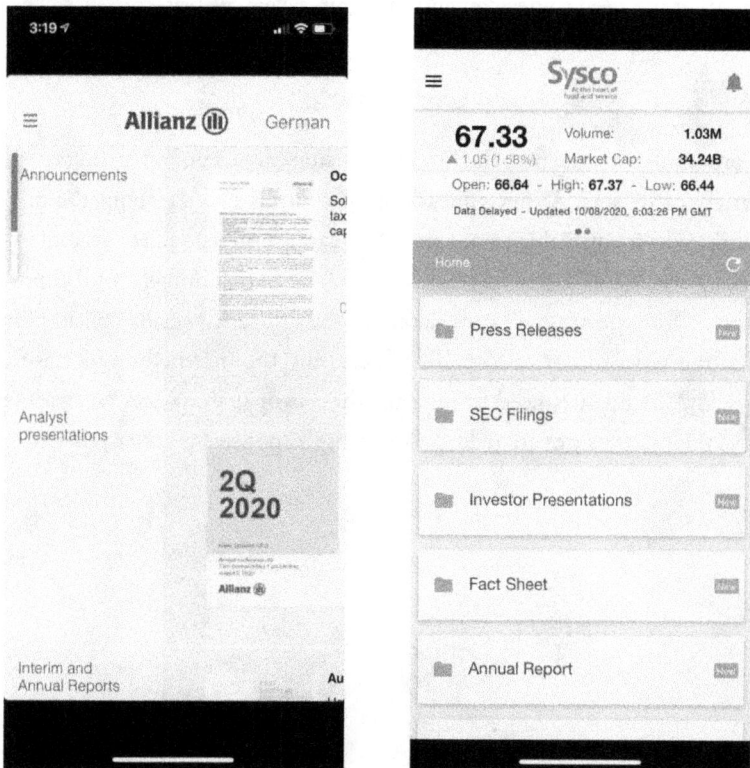

Figure 8.2 Investor apps on a smartphone

IR apps contain much or most of the information on the IR websites, including press releases, financials, SEC filings, investor presentations, etc. For phones, many of the documents, such as annual reports, are too large to be displayed on the screen. The result is that the print is too small for anyone to read. The print size can, of course, be expanded, but this results in the user being able to see only part of a page. For tablets, this size problem is not as much of an issue for users, since the screens are larger.

Numerous companies provide IR apps, including, for example, Sysco, Colgate, Allianz, Chevron, and Credit Suisse. The main advantage of apps as opposed to responsive websites is that they are easy to access and can be used offline to a degree. However, the difficulty of reading the larger documents on smartphones appears to have limited the numbers of companies providing these apps. The use of responsive websites is much more common, as the main website can be structured to be responsive, thus avoiding the need to develop and maintain several websites.

Conclusions

Corporate reporting over the Internet is being carried out on an increasing variety of devices. At one time, desktop computers were about the only kind of device available to people. Then came laptops, tablets and smartphones, with the latter increasing dramatically in numbers and importance. Other devices will come along in the future, especially considering that the types of devices capable of accessing the Internet are increasing quickly. Companies need to monitor the use of such devices and ensure that their disclosures are made in the most responsive manner possible.

CHAPTER 9

Environmental, Social, and Governance (ESG) Reporting

During the late 1980s, companies gradually began to report externally on their impacts on the environment and society. This voluntary reporting was partly in response to increasing demands from various nongovernmental organizations (NGOs) for corporate accountability with regard to environmental and social impacts and, partly from companies that wished to portray themselves as good corporate citizens and protect their reputations in the wake of serious environmental incidents in certain industries.

From the 1980s until the early 2000s, such reporting was most often called sustainability reporting. It attracted little attention from investors other than the relatively small number of "responsible" investors who used the information for screening their investments. To promote greater worldwide rigor and reliability for such reporting, in 2000 the Global Reporting Initiative (GRI) released its first Guidelines for Sustainability Reporting.

> GRI is an independent international organization that has pioneered sustainability reporting since 1997. GRI helps businesses and governments worldwide understand and communicate their impact on critical sustainability issues such as climate change, human rights, governance and social well-being.[1]

The Standards are developed with multistakeholder contributions and are rooted in the public interest. The GRI Sustainability Reporting Standards are the first and most widely adopted global standards for sustainability reporting. These evolved over the years and were widely adopted by large companies around the world, becoming the de facto standard for sustainability reporting.

It was not until the early 2000s, however, that the mainstream investment community, especially major public pension funds, began to consider that E, S, and G factors could materially affect a company's financial performance and future value to investors and indeed be material for sound investment decision-making. As firm empirical evidence grew, with strong academic backing, demand exploded for ESG type data that investors and analysts could use in planning and evaluating investment portfolios.

Sustainability reports proved inadequate as sources for this data, because their disclosures were designed to meet the broad information needs of stakeholders in general, not to present or highlight information material to investors. In 2005, the UN Global Compact coined the acronym ESG, and in 2006 the UN Principles of Responsible Investment organization was founded to promote institutional investment practices built on the integration of E, S, and G factors into the investment policies and decision making of signatory investment institutions.

ESG reporting continued to evolve and grow to meet the expectations of its broader audiences. A whole new data-driven industry thus emerged to fuel investors' ESG information needs, including ratings, data research and aggregation, such as Bloomberg terminals with downloadable data and spreadsheets for analysts.

Growth of ESG Reporting

Environmental reporting covers the interaction of enterprises with the environment. This is well documented and involves both the impact of enterprise activities on the environment (oil spills, air pollution, etc.) and the impact of the environment on company activities (floods, tornados, etc.). Social reporting covers social issues like a company's labor practices, talent management, product safety, and data security. Lack of proper data security, for example, has caused some companies considerable embarrassment and money when customer data was compromised. Governance reporting covers matters like board diversity, executive pay, and business ethics. Companies often have a governance committee of the Board of Directors to monitor governance policy and procedures.

The interest in and need for ESG Reporting has been augmented by numerous events, including:

1. Between 1980 and 2020, NOAA reported "117 Severe Storm, 17 Wildfire, 45 Tropical Cyclone, 33 Flooding, 27 Drought, 17 Winter Storm, and 9 Freeze billion-dollar disaster events affected the United States."[2]

2. In March 2020, powerful tornadoes caused considerable damage in and around Nashville, affecting many homes, businesses, vehicles, 90 planes and numerous buildings at the Nashville airport. There was also additional hail and wind damage in surrounding states. The cost was $1.1 billion.

3. In January 2020, more than 80 tornadoes and severe storms caused damage across many southeastern states. Storms and severe flooding also impacted several northern states. Significant damage occurred along the shoreline of Lake Michigan, to roads, the foundations of homes, and to Port Milwaukee. Powerful waves were generated by high winds and a lack of seasonal ice cover. The cost was estimated as $1.1 billion.

4. In the summer and fall of 2019, California experienced a damaging wildfire season, largely resulting from the Kincade and Saddle Ridge wildfires. In addition, Alaska suffered a near-historic wildfire season with more than 2.5 million acres burned. These wildfire conditions were primed due to Alaska's record-breaking heat and dry conditions during the summer months. The cost was estimated at $4.5 billion.

5. Examples abound of data breaches that have been very costly for companies. In 2013, Adobe reported that hackers had stolen 38 million user IDs and encrypted passwords. Later it turned out to be more than 150 million username and password pairs. Ultimately, Adobe had to pay $1.1 million in legal fees and $1 million to settle customer claims.[3]

6. In another case in 2016, Yahoo suffered what was touted as the biggest data breach in history. The attackers compromised the names, passwords, e-mail addresses, birth dates, and telephone numbers of 500 million users. Later that year, Yahoo disclosed another breach from 2013 by a different attacker that compromised, they said,

the details of 1 billion user accounts. In 2017, they revised that estimate to all of its 3 billion user accounts. The breaches knocked an estimated $350 million off the value of the company when it was sold that year.

"Almost two-thirds of the world's institutional investors are concerned about the impact of cyber security threats on their investments, making it investors' foremost environmental, social and governance (ESG) risk," according to the 2019 RBC Global Asset Management Responsible Investment Survey.

With these and other occurrences, investors have become more aware that environmental, social, and governance issues can affect the performance of investment portfolios and should be considered alongside more traditional financial factors. They have also become more aware that these types of events do indeed have serious financial implications themselves.

Larry Fink, CEO of BlackRock—the largest asset manager in the country—made this point in his annual letter to CEOs in 2018. Fink emphasized that companies must serve a social purpose. "To prosper over time," he writes, "every company must not only deliver financial performance, but also show how it makes a positive contribution to society."[4]

Companies have responded by releasing growing numbers of ESG reports, which are usually included in their websites, although the governmental aspect is often included as a separate report, either in the IR section of the website or in a separate section of the website.

Standards for ESG Reporting

With the growth in ESG reporting and its increased importance to investors and others, the issue of standards became more important. In 2011, the Sustainability Accounting Standards Board (SASB) was created as a U.S. NGO to develop standards for voluntary ESG disclosures by companies in their 10-K filings, especially MD&As, that is, disclosures that would be considered material under the SEC definition for materiality.

The Sustainability Accounting Standards Board is a progeny of the SASB Foundation, a nonprofit organization set up by a group of prominent businesses and individuals in the United States to help businesses around the world "identify, manage and report on the sustainability topics that matter most to their investors." SASB standards differ by industry, enabling investors and companies to compare performance from company to company within an industry, and are developed based on extensive feedback from companies, investors, and other market participants as part of a transparent, publicly documented process. Compliance with SASB pronouncements has increased in recent years, driven in part by the demands of stakeholders who recognize the tremendous financial impact of environmental disasters and issues.

In 2016, after five years of working with investors, companies, and other experts, SASB issued standards for use by companies in over 70 industry sectors, in order to enhance the comparability and usefulness of ESG disclosures. The SASB standards have the potential to be applicable in all international jurisdictions, not just in the United States, and are therefore to be key to meeting investor needs.

Because of the perceived threat of climate change to the stability of worldwide financial systems and institutions, the Financial Stability Board under Mark Carney created an international Task Force on Climate-related Financial Disclosures (TCFD) to meet investor information needs. In 2017, the TCFD released its recommendations for disclosures by financial institutions and companies about governance, strategy, risk (physical, liability, and transition-related), metrics and targets. Pressure is mounting in all major economies and jurisdictions to adopt, implement, and enforce TCFD-specified climate disclosures as a core element of information needed by responsible investors.

The FSB TCFD develops voluntary, consistent climate-related financial risk disclosures for use by companies in providing information to investors, lenders, insurers, and other stakeholders. The Task Force considers the physical, liability, and transition risks associated with climate change and what constitutes effective financial disclosures across industries.

These sustainability and ESG reporting initiatives and standards have two things in common:

1. their need for and dependence on a very wide variety of data-types and enormous quantities of data, plus the technologies for both companies and report/data users to handle this, and
2. the opportunity for reporting companies to use Internet and website technologies (including data tagging such as XBRL) effectively for presenting information and making it accessible and "friendly" to users.

Because of these commonalities, information technology is an essential enabler today for both providers and users of sustainability reporting and ESG disclosures, including TCFD-guided climate reporting.

The European Commission (EC) continued making headway on nonfinancial reporting with an announcement in 2020 that the European Financial Reporting Advisory Group (EFRAG) would develop recommendations for nonfinancial reporting standards. EFRAG is mobilizing a balanced and broad task force, taking into account a wide range of stakeholders and expertise, to prepare technical advice. The recommendations must build on existing standards and frameworks, and will be developed in close association with existing standard setting organisations.[5]

In 2020, PriceWaterhouseCoopers released a report[6] that offers some guidance on how businesses can recognize their responsibilities for information beyond the purely financial. They suggested that:

1. Global connectivity and local initiative must go hand-in-hand.
   Increasingly corporate performance is measured globally. However, their work has major impacts on local communities. Overall objectives and initiatives need to be aligned between global objectives and local community objectives.
2. Look beyond financial performance
   Corporate performance has traditionally been measured on financial results only. It rings hollow to certain communities,

however, when a company announces that it has achieved record profits but has closed several plants, some of which were the life-blood of those communities. Over recent years, some change in corporate reporting has been made. Corporate performance has increasingly included sustainability reporting that focuses on impact on the environment. That's great, and is starting to have a positive impact on corporate behavior. Corporate reporting has also been expanded to include ESG, but it is questionable whether the change in behavior has extended to the impact on society and communities. The reporting has, in many cases, but there is much more to be done. Companies can't be totally responsible for those communities, but they can be held responsible for significant actions they take that impact on the communities.

3. Technology doesn't care. But we must.

Technology is people neutral. If people are harmed by the effect of technology in a corporation, only the management and other people in the corporation can help direct that effect to as positive a result as possible.

4. Educate for the future

Education and retraining must be a responsibility of the companies involved. They are often the first to see the need for new skills and the opportunities for education to develop those skills. They need to play a role in meeting the needs of the future.

An explanation of these guidelines is included in the PWC report.[7] It is clear that significant change is required in corporate reporting. More emphasis on ESG reporting is essential as well as more Integrated Reporting.

Are the Standards Adequate?

According to GRI, Sustainability reporting is now common practice among upwards of 5,000 of the world's largest companies, and two-thirds of these companies are reporting in line with the GRI Standards. Even when they are presented in corporate websites, however, most sustainability disclosures are currently "locked" into PDF reports, which means their usage is somewhat restricted to reading them and copying the details into a form that can be analyzed. The PDF form not only makes assessment to improve decision making more cumbersome, it also makes comparison between companies more difficult.

Moving toward data-centric digital reporting would help companies respond more easily to information requests from data users, reduce the inaccuracies of data mining from pdf reports, and address the growing demand for sustainability information from stock exchanges, governments, investors, and consumers.

The standards, particularly those of the GSI, have made a strong contribution to the quality and consistency of the environmental reports released by companies. In addition, the GRI standards include guidance on making materiality decisions for ESG reports, which is different from making materiality decisions for financial information, although both are based on the same basic principle—that which is likely to influence decisions can be deemed to be material.

Companies Reporting on ESG

Eco-Act performs studies every year of companies reporting on ESG issues. In their report on 2018, they listed the top 10 companies worldwide from the CAC 40, DOW 30, FTSE 100, and IBEX 35. Information Technology and Telecommunications companies topped the IBEX, FTSE, and DOW. Energy, water, and multiutilities companies are also heavily represented, taking up four of the top 10 places.

The top three were Microsoft, BT Group, and Marks & Spencer.

- Microsoft (https://microsoft.com/en-us/corporate-responsibility)
  Microsoft has an extensive report on their website on ESG matters. It includes disclosures on privacy, particularly as it pertains to customer data, developing skills for employability of people, environmental matters such as water preservation and recycling, and the use of technology for helping non profits. The site also has other related material, books, and reference materials for further information.

- BT Group (https://btplc.com/Sharesandperformance/index. htm)

  BT, originally British Telecom, has an outstanding ESG report. Titled "Digital Impact and Sustainability Report", it has sections on the corporate digital initiatives on digital rights, and tackling climate change and environmental Challenges. The reporting by BT has won numerous awards, including a gold medal for seven straight years.

- Marks & Spencer is a good example of ESG reporting but a better example of Integrated Reporting, as discussed in the next chapter. For ESG, see (https://marksandspencer.com/c/ make-it-matter)

  Their ESG report is comprehensive, focusing on the care taken by the company to ensure the products it handles in its stores conform to high sustainability standards. For example, there is a whole section on the use of cotton in the clothing it sells, their efforts to be carbon neutral and their support of veganism.

Conclusions

There are a great many companies around the world reporting on ESG matters because of the widespread conclusion of the importance of E, S, and G. This recognition has led to the conclusion that ESG reporting may not be going far enough, and that there needs to be greater recognition in corporate reporting that ESG and Financial considerations are closely related and intertwined. The result has been a greater interest in integrated reporting, the subject of the next chapter.

In the next chapter, we will examine the evolution of Integrated Reporting to connect sustainability and ESG information with financial information and intangibles to provide a holistic view of how companies create value for stakeholders, including investors, and the essential roles of the Internet and company websites as well as data collection and management technologies in this process.

CHAPTER 10

Integrated Reporting

The origins of integrated reporting can be traced as far back as the 1990s when Kaplan & Norton came up with the idea of the balanced scorecard[1] to present a comprehensive, multidimensional view of the financial and nonfinancial drivers of value creation by a company.

Progressive large companies, mostly European-based such as Phillips and Novo Nordisk, began to explore how to embed into their business models, the strategic thinking and planning that they believed were central drivers of or contributors to business success, competitive advantage, resilience, stakeholder trust, and long-term value creation.

Such thinking, accompanied by new metrics and balanced scorecards, was conducive to improved management decision making, and also called for deeper, more formal, systematic stakeholder engagement to identify issues important to a company's success. These companies saw this as an important step forward from just carrying out regulatory compliance and corporate social responsibility programs.

It also followed that such companies would lead the way in experimenting with progressive reporting, by including in their annual reports and websites the information about those aspects of their environmental and social performance, policies, and targets which they saw as fundamentally linked to their overall business and performance, financial results, and prospects for future value creation.

Presenting these financial and nonfinancial types of information together, connected in one report, would, they believed, be more effective in communication with stakeholders than just separate, stand-alone sustainability or CSR reports, and would also, like a good MD&A, help investors and analysts understand with greater insight the context for and broad spectrum of value drivers behind a company's reported financial results and future prospects. The stage was set for wider experimentation and development of what we call today integrated reporting.

A milestone event occurred in 2010 when, following discussions convened by HRH Prince Charles, the Global Reporting Initiative joined forces with Accounting for Sustainability (a UK charity sponsored by the Prince) to create the International Integrated Reporting Council (later renamed Committee) in order to advance integrated reporting worldwide as a mainstream reporting practice and develop a framework to guide companies in producing integrated reports.

After issuing a Discussion Paper in 2011, and a Consultation Draft early in 2013, the International Integrated Reporting Council (IIRC)[2] released its international framework for integrated reporting in December 2013. The IIRC is now a global coalition of regulators, investors, companies, standard setters, the accounting profession, academia, and non-profit organizations that are independent of governments (NGOs). Its mission is to establish integrated reporting and thinking as a part of mainstream business practice.

The IIRC Integrated Reporting Framework is based on some fundamental concepts, some reporting principles, and recommended content elements, for an integrated report. Selecting and designing metrics for disclosing a company's use of, and impacts on, human, intangible, social, and natural capital is a major challenge and a work-in-progress.

The advent of integrated reporting does not mean that financial statements and sustainability/ ESG reports are suddenly obsolete. On the contrary, shareholders and investors will certainly continue to expect periodic IFRS financial statements, perhaps with an MD&A (Management Commentary in IASB lingo); broader types of stakeholders will certainly continue to seek the more detailed sustainability information they receive in sustainability reports; while institutional investors, fund managers, and analysts will expect material ESG disclosures and TCFD-based climate disclosures that will not be included in a concise integrated report.

Traditional paper-based reporting becomes very cumbersome in this new reporting environment and does not readily facilitate the needs of users who seek insights into the connections between different content elements and formats. Thanks to developments in website technology, hyperlinks, and data tagging, companies can readily link their core integrated reports with supplementary reports and data sets that users can custom select and download as they choose. Indeed, one whole chapter in "One Report: Integrated Reporting for a Sustainable Strategy" (Eccles and Krzus, Wiley, 2010) is devoted to The Internet and Integrated Reporting. Consider the advances in Internet, website, and data management technologies and user devices since 2010!

Integrated reporting is reporting that includes financial and ESG (environmental, social, and governance) reporting in one single report. It involves more than simply combining those separate reports into one report, but rather is a process of actually integrating the disclosures so that the financial, social, environmental, and governance implications of the various disclosures are all discussed together. In other words, suppose there has been a fire at one of the manufacturing plants and all materials used for manufacturing have been destroyed. The materials included paint and chemicals that emitted toxic fumes into the atmosphere. As a result, nearby residents had to evacuate for several days. The financial loss on this fire would be disclosed in the usual manner. The environmental implications in terms of the resultant pollution and how it was dealt with would be disclosed as well. In addition, the social implications might include the extent and nature of the disruption to the community that ensued, as well as the actions taken to remedy this for the residents. Finally, the governance implications might include a review of any governmental failings that might have led to the fire as well as any remedial action taken, such as regular inspections by fire marshals or amendments to the governance structure as it applies to fire safety.

With integrated reporting, investors and others would be made fully aware of all the implications of the fire in one place.

Reading Differs from Analysis

The content of websites is still based on a variety of paper reports—financial statements, annual reports, MD&A, President's Report, and so on. At one time, people would receive these reports in the mail, open them at their desk or kitchen table, and read them from cover to cover, making notes along the way and then following up on any unanswered questions. If they wanted to compare a particular item, say sales revenue in the income statement, to what another report might say, such as the MD&A, they would make a note of the item, look it up in the MD&A and then read about it there, again making notes as necessary.

In the age of technology, people are less likely to read this way. More often, they will read in a nonlinear fashion, following particular items and ideas across the various reports, using hyperlinks and search engines. In the age of technology, information should be presented not just to recognize this approach, but to facilitate it.

Most corporate websites present their corporate reports in a PDF Format, which was designed to preserve the format and content of paper reports. They are intended to be read in the same way as paper reports were always read. They can accommodate hyperlinks, but there is very little hyperlinking of information in practice.

There is also very little presentation of interactive data, that is, data in HTML, XBRL, or other markup languages. Only sometimes are the financial statements presented in these languages. Some use HTML. And XBRL is required by the U.S. Securities and Exchange Commission. But, again, when the information is presented, it is usually based on the same format as the old paper reports. The emphasis is on the individual reports, not on the data or information they actually contain.

To further aggravate the situation, very few companies have adopted Integrated Reporting. At present, companies typically present financial reports and ESG (Environmental, Social, and Governance) reports separately. In addition, the governance reports and, sometimes, the social reports are often presented separately from the environmental reports.

The IIRC has been promoting the idea of Integrated Reporting (IR) for many years. They have made a lot of progress, but IR is still a long way from being generally accepted. IR requires that all the information in those reports would be presented in such a way that all aspects of a particular item or issue can be quickly absorbed by the readers. As the IIRC puts it, "an integrated report is a concise communication about how an organization's strategy, governance, performance and prospects, in the context of its external environment, lead to the creation of value in the short, medium and long term."[3]

Website Presentation

In *The Future of Corporate Reporting—Creating the Dynamics for Change*,[4] a study published by The Federation of European Accountants, the following point is made:

> The corporate reporting of the future should take full account of changes in technology. Developments in the model for future corporate reporting should be flexible and able to adapt to changes in technology which affect the way people interact with an entity and which significantly affect the delivery of the information itself.[5]

Taking full advantage of technology means, in part, moving away from the paper paradigm way of thinking, using the features offered by technology. With websites, those features include interactivity, hyperlinking, multimedia, availability, and the ability to report on a real-time basis. Of course, technology extends beyond websites. Most listed companies make some use of social media, although this varies widely in terms of the coverage of information and the specific social media outlets used. All the same, companies have been experimenting with social media. Companies have also been experimenting with the use of apps for conveying their financial and business information.

Apps are used primarily in tablets and smartphones, and are downloaded and installed on the user's device. They are very powerful in terms of the information they can provide. Examples of available apps are those offered by Walmart, Shell, Bank of Montreal, and Canadian Tire. All present a wide variety of investor-related information, often similar to that available on their websites.

> Most people would agree that technology has changed their way of working and living significantly. Current developments in technology and social media already bring an unprecedented level of immediacy and sharing of information. Accessibility of corporate reporting has extended to stakeholders well beyond the investment community that represents its historical target. Information published on websites and through other digital means is instantly available to global audiences.[6]

CORE & MORE

The Future of Corporate Reporting—Creating the Dynamics for Change suggested a new approach to corporate reporting, called CORE & MORE. This approach is based on a "building block" or a "layered" approach. Financial reporting, according to this new model, would have two distinct parts: a CORE Report, and additional information (MORE) provided and referenced from the CORE report to the supplementary layers of reporting.[7]

In concept, the CORE & MORE approach is quite simple. The CORE Report could be, for example, a short summary of the major events during a reporting period, along with the key performance indicators. That would give a reader an instant picture of the company's financial and business status at a very high level. Most companies already provide a summary like this on their Investor Relations webpage, under a heading such as "Highlights" or "Key Performance Indicators," although they do not use it as a CORE Report.

The MORE reports would come up through hyperlinks to the items in the CORE Report. For example, one key indicator would likely be Net Income, which would be in the CORE Report and hyperlinked to the MORE reports, which might include, say, the income statement and/or the operating results section of the MD&A. Or there could be all kinds of variations on this structure. The point is that the pyramid would start at a high-level report and then progress down to more and more detailed reports, perhaps even to basic data levels, although this is very rare at present.

The presentation of the CORE Report need not be restricted to the website. It could be placed in social media, complete with hyperlinks, thus making the report more available to the readership. Or it could be the core of an app that would be installed on a mobile device.

A follow-up paper, published by Accountancy Europe in 2017, documented the responses of various people and organizations. There was general support for the report and the CORE & MORE concept, although the point was made that "the CORE & MORE concept should be clarified, redefined, and further fine-tuned and explained how it relates to integrated reporting."

This perceived need for clarification came out of the sweeping nature of the "future" report and the application of the CORE & MORE concept. Along with the basic concept, *The Future of Corporate Reporting* stated that traditional financial statements were becoming less important, and that nonfinancial information was becoming more important and needed to be included in the CORE & MORE reports, as should the ESG reports usually given as separate reports.

Of course, this raises a number of issues. It also points to the need for companies to experiment to come up with the best reporting approach. And it points to the clear need for the standards-setting bodies to step up.

Reporting in the Future

Accountancy Europe's follow-up paper contained the following conclusion:

> Respondents and participants anticipate that corporate reporting will, amongst other things, be web-based in the future; meaning that we expect to gradually move away from the traditional paper/PDF format. Technology can enhance both the preparation and presentation of reports. Innovation could, for instance, result in a better overview of the information (structured reporting) and greater user-friendliness. Technology as such can be both a driver and enabler of change in corporate reporting.[8]

In a speech delivered at an Accountancy Europe event in Brussels in 2017,[9] the chair of the International Accounting Standards Board, Hans Hoogervorst, offered a response to the CORE & MORE reports.

While pointing out that traditional financial statements remain a crucial element of corporate reporting, because of their confirmatory role, nevertheless he acknowledged the need for change. In particular, he pointed to demands for more detail, more subheadings and more data. He also referred to the growing use of the IFRS taxonomy by regulators and intermediaries. This fact he correctly identified as evidence of the changing manner in which financial statements are being consumed. This goes back to the point that people do not read them sequentially any more but, rather, use them as a vehicle for exploring particular items of interest.

On the broader issues of corporate reporting outside of the financial statements, such as the role of nonfinancial information and ESG reporting, Hoogervorst acknowledged the importance of integrated reporting and the Integrated Reporting Framework as promulgated by the IIRC. That framework provides guidance on content but leaves a good bit of flexibility in how the Integrated Report is actually compiled. It does not provide answers on how to prepare CORE & MORE reports. Nevertheless, the idea of integrated reports has gained considerable traction and has been experimented with by numerous companies around the world.

With regard to ESG reporting, Hoogervorst stated that:

The CORE & MORE report rightly notes that the world of sustainability reporting does not provide the same kind of global comparability that exists in the world of financial reporting. The report calls for "decisive leadership" to establish an international standard-setter and even poses the question if the IASB as renowned international standard-setter should provide at least part of that leadership.[10]

He added that:

That ideal world is still far away, I am afraid. In the meantime we will have to make the best of the imperfect world of corporate reporting. The IASB is ready to adapt to the changing world of corporate reporting by increasing the communication effectiveness of the financial statements, facilitating electronic consumption of financial data and by promoting integrated reporting. I hope my contribution of today has made clear what the IASB can and cannot do to create a bit more clarity in this imperfect world.[11]

Companies that have experimented with the CORE & MORE approach include ABN AMBRO Bank of Amsterdam. The Netherlands is a leader in electronic reporting, and in particular in the use of XBRL. Tjeerd Krumpelman, Head of Advisory, Reporting & Engagement for the bank, in replying to a question as to what attracted the bank to CORE & MORE, said the following:

> We saw 3 things increasing: the number of regulatory requirements we had to comply with, the interest level in NFI, or pre-financial indicators as I like to call them from different stakeholder groups beyond investors, which then led to our integrated annual report's volume to rise to over 450 pages.
>
> We needed a targeted approach to more concisely tell our story and address the interests from different stakeholder groups. We like CORE & MORE because it gives the freedom to tell our true story: who we are and how we create value for stakeholders. It also allows us to do so in a concise, clear and understandable way and in less than 100 pages.[12]

Krumpelman pointed to two key issues in the current model of corporate reporting—the size of the reports and the ability to tell a company's own story independently of regulatory requirements.

Massimo Romano, Head of Group Integrated Reporting for Generali, an insurance company based in Trieste, Italy, hit the nail on the head:

> CORE & MORE fits in our aim for simpler, faster, and smarter corporate reporting: easier to manage, more effective in delivering and applying integrated thinking. It is really powerful to focus on the value creation story and the strategic information to connect the dots between reports, disclosing specific detailed information and break down siloes.[13]

Also, Romano went on to encourage: ". . . connecting the CORE & MORE concept to other relevant initiatives such as aligning it with the IASB's work on a management commentary framework."[14]

These commentators recognize that, if the aim is to provide understanding among corporate stakeholders, presenting simpler, shorter reports is the way to go. They also recognize that the standard setters should begin work on the disclosure and content standards for CORE & MORE reports. Also, these reports need to be audited, which means the profession should develop appropriate auditing standards and techniques for these reports.

Restructuring the corporate reporting model along these lines is a big job. But it is slowly happening because of the growth of reporting on the web. Gradually, hyperlinks and interactive data are growing in their use, and investors are relying on the information provided. It becomes a question of whether the accounting and auditing profession wants to have some control over the standards around the new form of reporting, or whether it is happy to watch them develop in an ad hoc way over the next several years.

Other companies that have tried Integrated Reporting so far include:

a. Vodacom (http://vodacom-reports.co.za/integrated-reports/ir-2019/)

   Vodacom provides integrated reports (Figure 10.1) both as a separate file for download from its website and online. The reports incorporate summary financial statements, governance information, and some sustainability information. They also provide

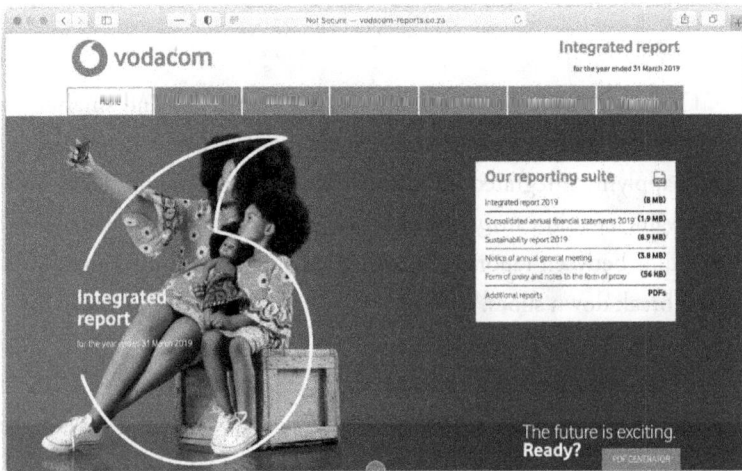

Figure 10.1 Vodacom integrated report

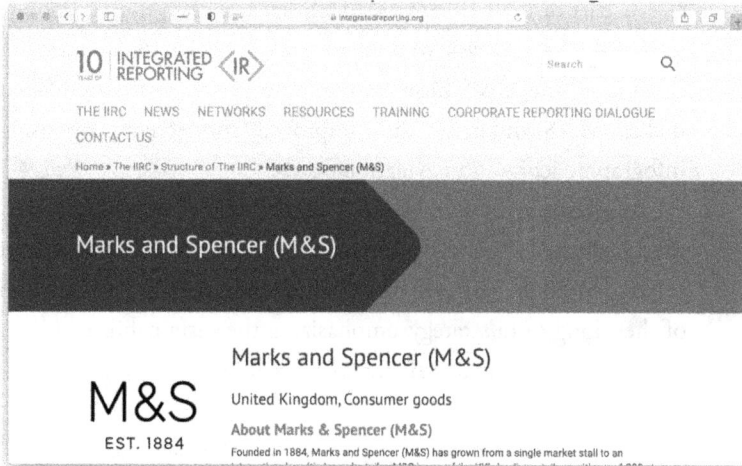

Figure 10.2 Marks & spencer integrated report

separate financial and sustainability reports. This is indicative of the state of integrated reporting, in that various companies are experimenting with the concept. The result is that there are vast differences in the reports provided by different companies.

b. Marks & Spencer

M&S joined the Integrated Reporting Pilot Programme with IIRC (Figure 10.2). After participating in that programme, they committed to an Annual Report to meet the IR principles by 2016. The company formed an IR Working Party to support that work, participated in the IR Business Network and consulted with Deloitte for guidance.

As the company announced,

M&S supports the IIRC's acknowledgement that IR is a journey, and that the IR principles provide a framework and a guide, rather than a list of prescriptive rules for an organisation to become integrated. We have recognised the need to give careful consideration as to how to apply the principles of IR to our own business model to ensure that communications remain relevant for our stakeholders.[15]

As part of their IR efforts, M&S strengthened their corporate responsibility and risk disclosures and in 2014/15 focussed on developing the M&S business model to clearly articulate "What makes M&S different" and improved connectivity by using infographic icons and navigational aids.

In addition, in accordance with the UK Governance Code, they included a Viability Statement within their Annual Report starting in 2016. This was designed to strengthen the articulation of their long-term strategy, emphasizing the sustainability of their value creation—a major element of integrated reporting.

c. British Land

The British Land integrated report for 2019 is found at https://britishland.com/~/media/Files/B/British-Land-V4/documents/ar-2019/reporting-centre/annual-report-and-accounts-2019.pdf

As noted in that report,

We integrate social and environmental information throughout this Report in line with the International Integrated Reporting Framework. This reflects how sustainability is integrated into our placemaking strategy, governance and business operations. Our industry-leading sustainability strategy is a powerful tool to deliver lasting value for all our stakeholders.

The report is a prime example of integrated reporting.

In 2015 the IIRC convened what they called a "Corporate Reporting Dialogue" among leading global corporate reporting standard setters and regulators. It aims for collaboration in cutting through what it calls the jungle and the ensuing reporting clutter, by suggesting the adoption of Integrated Reporting.

Integrated Web-Based Reporting

The main pros of integrated reporting center around the idea that investors and other stakeholders have a significant stake in the nonfinancial aspects of corporate reporting, including particularly ESG. Moreover, they need to know how the ESG aspects affect the financial aspects, and vice versa. The traditional form of reporting always presented these elements of information as silos, but that no longer meets the needs of stakeholders. Integrated reporting provides a concise portrayal of all the interactions of the company with its environment and leads to a much better understanding of the effects of those interactions.

The idea of integrated reporting has special appeal for web-based reporting, since the Web is ideally suited to achieve it. This could be accomplished by turning much of the IR section of the website into an integrated report. All of the elements are already on the website, and are therefore available for integration. As we have noted, the existence of those elements does not make an integrated report, but rather simply a combined report. In fact, the elements are normally not combined but rather simply presented in proximity to each other. The process of integration might include adding or deleting items based on judgments about relevance and materiality.

On the con side, integrated reports can take extra time to prepare, and time is already short in preparing the traditional reports, particularly those required for regulatory reports. A great deal of extra planning is required to prepare the reports, with greater collaboration between various departments of the company.

If the prime reports are not integrated themselves, but rather a separate integrated report prepared, then the additional time can be wasted, since there will be a tendency for people to concentrate on the traditional reports. Moreover, in cases where this approach is taken, there is a tendency for the integrated report to be presented in summary form, which degrades the importance of the EG factors. Overall, all of the main reports need to be integrated in order to be effective.

Focusing on integrated reporting in considering the future of corporate reporting gives us a framework for considering the direction that web-based reporting is likely to take. Since web-based reporting has become the primary vehicle of corporate reporting, then this really sheds a lot of light on the future of corporate reporting itself. Integrated reporting both simplifies the reporting and at the same time makes it much more useful.

Summary and Conclusions

In this book, we have explored the use of the Internet for corporate reporting from its beginnings with the start of the World Wide Web up to the present, a period of approximately twenty-five years. Numerous changes have taken place during that period, some of which relate to the technology and others that relate to the changing business and reporting environment.

Changes in the technology have involved a massive increase in the power of computers and a shift to the use of the cloud for information technology purposes. Changes in the reporting environment have involved recognition that corporate reporting has to be directed to more than just financial issues toward environmental, social, and governance issues. This has led to a broadening of the scope of corporate reporting. There has also been an increased involvement of regulators and legislators in the reporting process.

All listed companies in the twenty-first century have websites and almost all of them include comprehensive financial information on those websites—often under the heading of "Investor Relations" or simply "Investors" or "Investor Information"—and this disclosure is widely acknowledged as a major source of information for corporate stakeholders. The websites don't replace the traditional information, like financial statements, MD&A and news releases; rather, they incorporate this information in the new and different communications vehicle—the World Wide Web.

When the World Wide Web became a viable vehicle for the sharing of information, corporate reporting was still largely fixed in the old style of reporting, one which was primarily limited to the presentation of financial statements and related commentary on paper. This style has been referred to as the paper paradigm.

The paper paradigm way of thinking carried forward into the years when reporting shifted to the World Wide Web, which meant that the production of traditional financial statements remained the core of the reporting process. Moreover, these financial statements were designed to be read, with any analysis to be done as a separate exercise where data is extracted from the financial statements and then entered into spreadsheets and other analytical tools.

Since the financial statements were designed to be read like a book, they were often presented in the corporate websites in PDF format, the format that is intended to preserve attractive and readable formats, but is not a good format for extracting data for analysis. After a few years, some companies began to compensate for this shortcoming by also presenting the statements in spreadsheet or HTML format, thus making the analysis of data much easier.

Still later, regulators began requiring the presentation of financial statements in XBRL format. The U.S. Securities and Exchange Commission was one of the early adopters of XBRL and the most influential. Requirements were introduced sporadically for the XBRL Statements to be presented on the corporate websites, but the most effective and useful requirement was for them to be presented in the regulators' websites. In the case of the SEC, this meant the statements were presented on the EDGAR system, which made the financial statements of all major listed companies readily available in a form that could be used easily for analysis. Presentation of financial information on such systems, in addition to the corporate websites, is considered to be a part of corporate reporting on the Internet.

Reporting on the Internet also includes the use of social media, which many companies have been using, although in differing degrees. Twitter is widely used to get quick messages out, such as dividend and stock change announcements. YouTube is often used for videos of events like executive speeches, shareholder meetings, and other events. Several other social media outlets are often used to some extent.

In addition to the presentation of videos, the Internet is also ideal for the presentation of graphics and multimedia. Most companies are making some use of this capability, although they are falling far short of the full capability of the Internet in this respect. Consequently, the graphics presentations one sees on corporate websites are often very much the same as one would see on paper. And so, again, the paper paradigm survives!

The use of various devices for accessing the Internet also has an impact on corporate reporting. For the most part, these include smartphones and tablets, which are characterized by smaller screens and computing capacity that is more limited than that of laptops and desk model computers. This means that websites need to be presented in responsive ways, such that they can be easily viewed on small screens. Most companies are taking this approach.

Through all this, the paper paradigm has proven to be quite resilient, with most companies still primarily using PDF to present their financial statements in their websites, although the presentations in alternative formats have also grown in usage.

While companies have been grappling with the presentation of financial statements on their websites, a major change has been taking place in the world of financial management: the shift toward data-driven decision making. While much of this shift has taken place in the realm of management decisions, nevertheless the purpose of financial statements is to be useful in the making of decisions. That means using them for data-driven decision making is made more difficult if they are presented in a form to be read rather than used for analysis.

Reporting on the Internet, however, began to adapt to data-driven decision making in a more direct way; by reporting arrays of data in tabular format using Excel or external data display tools. It is expected that such reporting will increase in the next few years and as it becomes more common, likely the regulators will leap into action. Another aspect of data reporting is that of reporting key performance indicators. This had been a regular practice for years, but the increased attention given to reporting data has resulted in some of that data being reported in the form of key performance indicators as well.

In addition to reporting data, a major societal shift toward growing concern about the environment, social issues, and governance issues resulted in an expansion of corporate reporting to encompass these areas. ESG reporting has been reflected in Internet reporting, usually in the form of silos. In most contemporary websites, environmental and social disclosures are included as a separate report. Governance disclosures are usually a part of the Annual Report, but are sometimes a separate report on the website.

Recent research indicates that all financial, environmental, social, and governance disclosures should be integrated into a general Integrated Report. Experience tells us that ESG elements have financial implications, and that many financial results are influenced by ESG. They cannot be separated, but that is what most companies do. The Internet offers a unique opportunity to present their results on an integrated basis. Most companies are missing this opportunity.

Notes

Introduction

1. (Hindi and Rich Winter 2010).
2. Ibid.
3. Website Posting of SEC and Corporate Governance Materials— Required Postings and Practical Advice. July 14, 2006. https://perkinscoie.com/en/news-insights/website-posting-of-sec-and-corporate-governance-materials.html
4. IFRS Foundation Trustees consult on global approach to sustainability reporting and on possible Foundation role, September 30, 2020, https://ifrs.org/news-and-events/2020/09/ifrs-foundation-trustees-consult-on-global-approach-to-sustainability-reporting/

Chapter 1

1. (ESG in the Boardroom February 2019).
2. (Thinking Allowed, The Future of Corporate Reporting 2016).
3. (D'Onofrio May 30, 2018).
4. Ibid.
5. Ibid.

Chapter 2

1. https://ifrs.org/issued-standards/list-of-standards/conceptual-framework/
2. (IR Magazine February 19, 2020).
3. https://businessroundtable.org/business-roundtable-redefines-the-purpose-of-a-corporation-to-promote-an-economy-that-serves-all-americans

Chapter 3

1. https://irmagazine.com
2. (Pendley 2008).
3. Ibid.
4. Ibid.

Chapter 4

1. (Understanding the 3 Vs of big data—volume, velocity, and variety, written by whishworks August 9, 2017).
2. Ibid.
3. (How Much Data Do We Create Every Day? May 28, 2018).
4. (Sargent October 21, 2019).
5. (Ankorion November 29, 2018).
6. https://whishworks.com/blog/big-data/understanding-the-3-vs-of-big-data-volume-velocity-and-variety
7. (Al-Htaybat and von Alberti-Alhtaybat 2017).
8. https://aplusmag.goodbarber.app/topics/c/0/i/17867251/big-data-big-impact-accounting
9. (Provost and Fawcett n.d.).
10. (Rezaee and Wang December 2017).
11. https://teck.com/investors/interactive-analyst-centre/
12. https://apps.indigotools.com/IR/IAC/?Ticker=RGEN&Exchange=NASDAQGS
13. https://apps.indigotools.com/IR/iac/?ticker=NTR&exchange=NYSE
14. http://apps.indigotools.com/IR/IAC/?Ticker=aem&Exchange=tsx#
15. https://apps.indigotools.com/IR/IAC/?Ticker=RGEN&Exchange=NASDAQGS#

Chapter 5

1. XBRL International, http://xbrl.org
2. David Blaszkowsky in an SEC Webinar recorded on https://sec.gov/rss/xbrl/interactive_data1.htm
3. https://ec.europa.eu/info/sites/info/files/business_economy_euro/banking_and_finance/documents/191128-ceaob-guidelines-auditors-involvement-financial-statements_en.pdf

Chapter 6

1. (Beattie and Jones 2008).
2. Adapted from the out of print Research Report "Practical Guidance for Preparing Graphics," Canadian Institute of Chartered Accountants, June 2008.
3. https://bluecorona.com/blog/social-video-marketing-trend/
4. (Kim, Oh, and Shin Summer 2010).
5. (Cho, Michelon, and Patten 2012).
6. (Beattie and Jones 2008).
7. Ibid.

Chapter 7

1. (Spaul September 1997).
2. The 2009 Social Media Reality Check consisted of two separate online surveys. The first survey, covering 1,516 respondents, was conducted among members of Leger Marketing Online Panel of adult residents from across Canada. (With a sample size of 1,516, results can be considered accurate to within ± 2.5 percentage points, 19 times out of 20.) The second survey, covering 615 respondents, was conducted with marketing/communications practitioners obtained primarily from CNW Group client lists. (With a sample size of 615, results can be considered accurate to within ± 4.0 percentage points, 19 times out of 20.) Both groups were identified to be users of social media. The survey results are available online at SlideShare.
3. Refer to "Survey Reveals IR Professionals Slowly Embrace Social Media, Especially Smaller Companies—and Which IR Blogs They Read."
4. (Abdel-Fattah May 6, 2015).
5. Read the December 3, 2009 article "Attention Twitter Fence Sitters: New Report Shows IR Twitter Usage Up; Q4 CEO Says Best Buy's IR 2.0 Best Practices Instructive" at *IR Alert* online.
6. Q4 Study in 2013.
7. Diageo and BP Top Social Media Reporting Index, *IR Magazine*, https://irmagazine.com/reporting/diageo-and-bp-top-social-media-reporting-index
8. Making a Splash with Financial Reporting on Social Media, https://fticonsulting.com/insights/fti-journal/making-splash-financial-reporting-social-media
9. (Chodor February 7, 2019).
10. SEC Press Release 2013–51, Washington, DC., April 2, 2013.
11. Pew Research Study.
12. GlobalWebIndex, Q1 2013 Stream Social report.

Chapter 8

1. (Walker November 19, 2019).
2. Ibid.
3. (Abdel-Fattah March 27, 2015).
4. (Financial Advisors leading users of tablets in business setting (Study), Q4, August 30, 2012).
5. (Mobile Fact Sheet, Pew Research June 5, 2019).
6. (The Future is Mobile Part 2: Best Practice Examples: Responsive Design February 19, 2014).
7. Ibid.
8. (Mobile Technology and its Growing Influence on IR Communication (Part 1), October 24, 2012).

Chapter 9

1. https://globalreporting.org/information/about-gri/Pages/default.aspx
2. https://ncdc.noaa.gov/billions/events
3. (Swinhoe April 17, 2020).
4. https://csoonline.com/article/2130877/the-biggest-data-breaches-of-the-21st-century.html
5. (ESG in the boardroom: What directors need to know, PWC, February 2019).
6. (EFRAG tasked with proposing Non-financial Reporting Standards, July 10, 2020 by Editor).
7. https://xbrl.org/news/efrag-tasked-with-proposing-non-financial-reporting-standards/(July 2020)
8. https://pwc.com/gx/en/issues/trust/common-purpose.html
9. Ibid.

Chapter 10

1. (Norton September 1, 1996).
2. https://integratedreporting.org/the-iirc-2/
3. http://integratedreporting.org
4. *The Future of Corporate Reporting—Creating the Dynamics for Change* (Brussels: Accountancy Europe, 2016).
5. Ibid, p. 17.
6. Ibid.
7. Ibid, p. 58.
8. Follow-up paper:-*The Future of Corporate Reporting* (Brussels: Accountancy Europe, March 2017), p. 5.
9. https://ifrs.org/news-and-events/2017/09/iasb-chairmans-speech-the-times-the-are-achangin/
10. Ibid.
11. Ibid.
12. *CORE & MORE in Practice Testimonials* (Brussels: Accountancy Europe, 2017).
13. Ibid.
14. Ibid.
15. https://integratedreporting.org/profile/marks-and-spencer-group-plc/

Bibliography

"EFRAG Tasked with Proposing Non-financial Reporting Standards." July 10, 2020 by Editor "ESG in the Boardroom: What Directors Need to Know." February 2019. PWC.

"Financial Advisors Leading Users of Tablets in Business Setting (Study), Q4." August 30, 2012. https://q4blog.com/2012/08/30/financial-advisors-leading-users-of-tablets-in-business-setting-study

"IFRS Foundation Trustees Consult on Global Approach to Sustainability Reporting and on Possible Foundation Role." September 30, 2020, https://ifrs.org/news-and-events/2020/09/ifrs-foundation-trustees-consult-on-global-approach-to-sustainability-reporting/

"International Accounting Standards Board and the US Financial Accounting Standards Board." Conceptual Framework Joint Project. https://iasplus.com/en/projects/completed/framework/framework-joint

"Mobile Fact Sheet." *Pew Research*, June 5, 2019, https://pewresearch.org/internet/fact-sheet/mobile/#who-is-smartphone-dependent

"Mobile Technology and its Growing Influence on IR Communication (Part 1)." October 24, 2012. Q4blog.com

"The Future is Mobile Part 2: Best Practice Examples: Responsive Design." February 19, 2014. Q4blog.com

"Website Posting of SEC and Corporate Governance Materials—Required Postings and Practical Advice." July 14, 2006. https://perkinscoie.com/en/news-insights/website-posting-of-sec-and-corporate-governance-materials.html

2016. *The Future of Corporate Reporting—Creating the Dynamics for Change.* Brussels: Accountancy Europe.

2017. *CORE & MORE in Practice Testimonials.* Brussels: Accountancy Europe.

Abdel-Fattah, R. March 27, 2015. "Five Communication Trends that Will Positively Influence Your IR Efforts." Q4blog.com

Abdel-Fattah, R. May 6, 2015. "Research Reports the Extent of Social Media Influence on Investment Decisions." Available online on the Q4 Website, https://q4blog.com/2015/05/06/research-reports-the-extent-of-social-media-influence-on-investment-decisions/

Adapted from the out of print Research Report. June 2008. "Practical Guidance for Preparing Graphics." Canadian Institute of Chartered Accountants.

Al-Htaybat, K., and L. von Alberti-Alhtaybat. 2017. "Big Data and Corporate Reporting: Impacts and Paradoxes." *Accounting, Auditing & Accountability Journal* 30, no. 4, pp. 850–873.

Allowed, T. 2016. *The Future of Corporate Reporting.* Deloitte, https://www2.deloitte.com/content/dam/Deloitte/ch/Documents/audit/ch-en-audit-thinking-allowed-future-corporate-reporting.pdf

Ankorion, I. 2018. "Growing Data Volumes: Dynamic Business Requirements and Ever-Changing Technology." November 29, 2018. https://dataversity.net/growing-data-volumes-dynamic-business-requirements-ever-changing-technology/#, https://whishworks.com/blog/big-data/understanding-the-3-vs-of-big-data-volume-velocity-and-variety

Beattie, V., and M. Jones. 2008. "Corporate Reporting Using Graphs: A Review and Synthesis." *Journal of Accounting Literature* 27, pp. 71–110.

Canadian Securities Administrators (CSA). XBRL voluntary filing program.
- NI 51-102 *Continuous Disclosure Obligations,* Part 4, Financial Statements, and Part 9, Proxy Solicitation and Information Circulars.
- NI 51-102F1 *Management's Discussion and Analysis.*
- NI 51-102F2 Annual Information Form.

Canadian Institute of Chartered Acccountants (CICA). Now CPA Canada.
- *20 Questions Directors Should Ask about Management's Discussion and Analysis.* Toronto, 2003.
- *Building a Better MD&A: A Guide for Smaller Issuers.* 2007.
- *Chronology of CICA's Climate Change and Sustainability Initiatives.* CICA press release. Toronto, February 12, 2007.
- *CICA Handbook-Accounting* Section 1000, Financial Statement Concepts and Section 1400, General Standards of Financial Statement Presentation.
- *Environmental Costs and Liabilities: Accounting and Financial Reporting Issues.* 1993.
- *Impact of Technology on Financial and Business Reporting. 1999.*
- *Interactive Data — Building XBRL into Accounting Information Systems. 2007.*
- *Management's Discussion and Analysis: Guidance on Preparation and Disclosure. 2004.*
- *MD&A Disclosure about the Financial Impact of Climate Change and Other Environmental Issues. 2005.*
- *Reporting on Environmental Performance. 1994.*
- *Stakeholder Relationships, Social Capital & Business Value. 2003.*
- *Strategic Performance Monitoring and Management: Using Non-financial Performance Measures to Improve Corporate Governance. 1998.*
- *The Measurement of Shareholder Value Creation. 1998.*

Cho, C.H., G. Michelon and D.M. Patten. 2012. "Enhancement and Obfuscation through the Use of Graphs in Sustainability Reports, An International Comparison." *Sustainability Accounting, Management and Policy Journal* 3, no. 1, pp. 74–88.

Chodor, B. 2019. "How is Social Media Transforming Investor Relations?" February 7, 2019. https://westuc.com/en-us/blog/digital-communications/infographic-how-social-media-transforming-investor-relations-0

D'Onofrio, D. 2018. "Continuous Reporting: Has the Time Come to Jettison Quarterly Reports?"

Davey, H., and K. Homkajohn. February 2004. "Corporate Internet Reporting: An Asian Example." *Problems and Perspectives in Management.*

David Blaszkowsky in an SEC Webinar recorded on https://sec.gov/rss/xbrl/interactive_data1.htm

Diageo and BP. n.d. Top Social Media Reporting Index, *IR Magazine*, https://irmagazine.com/reporting/diageo-and-bp-top-social-media-reporting-index

Electronic Communications Disclosure Guidelines. 2003. http://tsx.com/en/pdf/ElectronicCommunications.pdf

Eppler, M.J., and J. Mengis. 2003. *A Framework for Information Overload Research in Organizations: Insights from Organization Science, Accounting, Marketing, MIS, and Related Disciplines.* Università della Svizzera italiana.

Eppler, M.J., and J. Mengis. 2004. "The Concept of Information Overload: A Review of Literature from Organization Science, Accounting, Marketing, MIS, and Related Disciplines." *The Information Society* 20, no. 5, pp. 325–344.

ESG in the Boardroom. February 2019. *What Directors Need to Know.* PWC.

Follow-up paper: March 2017. *The Future of Corporate Reporting*, 5. Brusels: Accountancy Europe.

GlobalWebIndex, Q1 2013 Stream Social Report.

Héroux, S. July 2006. "Website Content Management and Analysis: A Stakeholder and Contingency Perspective." Working Paper. Montreal: Université du Québec à Montréal.

Hindi, N.M., and J. Rich. 2010. "Financial Reporting on the Internet: Evidence from the Fortune 100." *Management Accounting Quarterly* 11, no. 2, p. 11.

Ho, S.S.M., and K.S. Wong. Spring 2004. "Investment Analysts' Usage and Perceived Usefulness of Corporate Annual Reports." *Corporate Ownership & Control* 1, no. 3, pp. 61–71.

HRH the Prince of Wales. n.d. "Accounting for Sustainability." Project at St. James's palace. December 6, 2006.

http://integratedreporting.org

https://aplusmag.goodbarber.app/topics/c/0/i/17867251/big-data-big-impact-accounting

https://bluecorona.com/blog/social-video-marketing-trend/

https://ec.europa.eu/info/sites/info/files/business_economy_euro/banking_ and_finance/documents/191128-ceaob-guidelines-auditors-involvement-financial-statements_en.pdf

https://ifrs.org/news-and-events/2017/09/iasb-chairmans-speech-the-times-the-are-achangin/

https://pwc.com/gx/en/issues/trust/common-purpose.html

https://xbrl.org/news/efrag-tasked-with-proposing-non-financial-reporting-standards/ (accessed July 2020).

International Federation of Accountants. August 2002. *Financial Reporting on the Internet*. New York.

Jones, M.J., and J.Z. Xiao. 2004. "Financial Reporting on the Internet by 2010: A Consensus View." *Accounting Forum* 28, pp. 237–263.

Kaplan, R.S., and D.P. Norton. September 1, 1996. *The Balanced Scorecard: Translating Strategy Into Action*. Harvard Business Press.

Kim, C., E. Oh, and N. Shin. 2010. "An Empirical Investigation of Digital Content Characteristics, Value, and Flow." *The Journal of Computer Information Systems* 50, no. 4, pp. 79–87.

Kshama, V.K., and K. Dutta. January 2006. "Corporate Reporting— Without Shades of Grey." *The Chartered Accountant*, pp. 975–982.

Lymer, A., R. Debreceny, G.L. Gray, and A. Rahman. 1999. *Business Reporting on the Internet*. London: International Accounting Standards Committee.

Maines, L.A., and J.M. Wahlen. December 2006. "The Nature of Accounting Information Reliability: Inferences from Archival and Experimental Research." *Accounting Horizons* 20, no. 4, pp. 399–425.

Making a Splash with Financial Reporting on Social Media, https:// fticonsulting.com/insights/fti-journal/making-splash-financial-reporting-social-media

Marr, B. 2018. "How Much Data Do We Create Every Day? The Mind-Blowing Stats Everyone Should Read." May 28, 2018, https://forbes.com/sites/ bernardmarr/2018/05/21/how-much-data-do-we-create-every-day-the-mind-blowing-stats-everyone-should-read/#35b86f760ba9

May 30, 2018, https://snaplogic.com/blog/continuous-reporting-has-the-time-come-to-jettison-quarterly-reports

PricewaterhouseCoopers LLP (PWC). 2006. *Best Practices for Corporate Blogs*. London, www.corporatereporting.com

- *Business Review: has it made a difference? A survey of the narrative reporting practices of the FTSE 350*. 2007.
- *Corporate reporting—a time for reflection*. 2007.
- *Corporate Reporting: Is It What Investment Professionals Expect?* 2007.
- *Narrative Reporting: Give yourself a head start*. 2007.

Pendley, J.A., and A. Rai. 2009. "Internet Financial Reporting: An Examination of Current Practice." *International Journal of Disclosure and Governance* 6, no. 2, pp. 89–105.

Pendley, J.A., and A. Rai. October 29, 2008. "Internet financial Reporting: An Examination of Current Practice." *International Journal of Disclosure and Governance* 6, no. 2, pp. 89–105.

Provost, F., and T. Fawcett. 2013. *Data Science And Its Relationship To Big Data And Data-Driven Decision Making.* New York University.

Pyman, T.A. August 2007. "Brave New World." *Charter*, pp. 28–30.

Read the December 3, 2009 Article "Attention Twitter Fence Sitters: New Report Shows IR Twitter Usage Up; Q4 CEO Says Best Buy's IR 2.0 Best Practices Instructive" at *IR Alert* online.

Refer to "Survey Reveals IR Professionals Slowly Embrace Social Media, Especially Smaller Companies — and Which IR Blogs They Read."

Rezaee, Z., and J. Wang. December 2017. "Big Data, Big Impact on Accounting: A Plus." XBRL International, http://xbrl.org

Ruggeri, C. February 19, 2020. "Activism, Guidance and Purpose: The IR issues on the Minds of CFOs." *IR Magazine.*

Sargent, J. 2019. "Organizations are Struggling to Perform Business Analytics on Growing Data Volumes." October 21, 2019. https://sdtimes.com/data/report-organizations-are-struggling-to-perform-business-analytics-on-growing-data-volumes/

Schiff, A. Autumn 1978. "Annual Reports in the United States: A Historical Perspective." *Accounting and Business Research.* pp. 279–282.

SEC Press Release 2013–51, Washington, DC. April 2, 2013.

Sinnett, W.M. January/February 2006. "A Revolution in Corporate Reporting?" *Financial Executive*, pp. 40–42.

Smith, B., and D. Peppard. December 2005. "Internet Financial Reporting: Benchmarking Irish PLCs against Best Practice." *Accountancy Ireland* 37, no. 6, pp. 22–24.

Smith, J.K. June 2007. "Evaluating the Boundaries of SEC Regulation." *Journal of Corporate Finance* 13, nos. (2–3), pp. 189–194.

Sortur, S. January 2006. "Financial Reporting on Internet." *The Chartered Accountant.* London: Tomorrow's Company, www.tomorrowscompany.com

Spaul, B. September, 1997. *Corporate Dialogue in the Digital Age.* The Institute of Chartered Accountants in England and Wales, London.

Swinhoe, D. 2020. "The 15 Biggest Data Breaches of the 21st Century." April 17, 2020 https://csoonline.com/article/2130877/the-biggest-data-breaches-of-the-21st-century.html

Trabelsi, S., R. Labelle, and C. Laurin. 2004. "The Management of Financial Disclosure on Corporate Websites: A Conceptual Model." *Canadian Accounting Perspectives* 3, no. 2, pp. 235–259.

Wagenhofer, A. October 2003. "Economic Consequences of Internet Financial Reporting." *Schmalenbach Business Review* 55.

Walker, M. November 19, 2019. *Americans Favor Mobile Devices Over Desktops and Laptops for Getting News*. Pew Research Center.

Whishworks. August 9, 2017. *Understanding the 3 vs of Big Data—Volume, Velocity and Variety*.

About the Author

Gerald Trites is a CPA with a history of writing and publishing. He was a partner in KPMG for twenty years, and a Professor of Accounting and Information Systems at St. Francis Xavier University in Nova Scotia, where he served as Director of the Schwartz School of Business. He also served for twelve years as Director of XBRL Canada. He has published twelve books and numerous articles and papers. As a Research Associate for the Canadian Institute of Chartered Accountants, (now CPA Canada) he led the development of several sections of the *CICA Handbook*, the source of Canadian accounting and auditing standards, and he served as chair of the Auditing Standards Board. He also served for several years as the lead judge in the electronic disclosure division of the Corporate Disclosure contest run by CPA Canada. He currently serves as Editor-in-Chief of *ThinkTWENTY20* magazine, a publication he and a colleague, Gundi Jeffrey, started in 2019 with the objective of publishing well-researched articles of substance.

Index

OTHER TITLES IN THE FINANCIAL ACCOUNTING, AUDITING, AND TAXATION COLLECTION

Mark Bettner, Bucknell University, Michael Coyne, Fairfield University, Editors

- *Tax Aspects of Corporate Division* by Eugene W. Seago
- *Accounting for Business* by Roger Hussey, and Audra Ong
- *Sustainability Performance and Reporting* by Irene M. Herremans
- *Applications of Accounting Information Systems* by David M Shapiro
- *Forensic Accounting and Financial Statement Fraud, Volume II* by Zabi Rezaee
- *A Non-Technical Guide to International Accounting* by Roger Hussey, and Audra Ong
- *Forensic Accounting and Financial Statement Fraud, Volume I* by Zabihollah Rezaee
- *The Tax Aspects of Acquiring a Business, Second Edition* by Eugene W. Seago
- *Corporate Governance in the Aftermath of the Financial Crisis, Volume III* by Zabihollah Rezaee
- *Corporate Governance in the Aftermath of the Financial Crisis. Volume IV* by Zabihollah Rezaee
- *The Story Underlying the Numbers* by Veena S. Iyer
- *Using Accounting & Financial Information, Second Edition* by Mark S. Bettner
- *Pick a Number, Second Edition* by Roger Hussey, and Audra Ong,

Announcing the Business Expert Press Digital Library

Concise e-books business students need for classroom and research

This book can also be purchased in an e-book collection by your library as

- a one-time purchase,
- that is owned forever,
- allows for simultaneous readers,
- has no restrictions on printing, and
- can be downloaded as PDFs from within the library community.

Our digital library collections are a great solution to beat the rising cost of textbooks. E-books can be loaded into their course management systems or onto students' e-book readers. The **Business Expert Press** digital libraries are very affordable, with no obligation to buy in future years. For more information, please visit **www.businessexpertpress.com/librarians**. To set up a trial in the United States, please email **sales@businessexpertpress.com**.

www.ingramcontent.com/pod-product-compliance
Lightning Source LLC
Chambersburg PA
CBHW061327220326
41599CB00026B/5076